BASIC ANTHROPOLOGY UNITS

GENERAL EDITORS

George and Louise Spindler

STANFORD UNIVERSITY

PEASANTS IN COMPLEX SOCIETY

Detail from Jean François Millet's The Man with the Hoe *(1849)*.

FREDERICK C. GAMST
Rice University

Peasants in Complex Society

HOLT, RINEHART AND WINSTON, INC.
New York   Chicago   San Francisco   Atlanta
Dallas   Montreal   Toronto   London   Sydney

Library of Congress Cataloging in Publication Data

Gamst, Frederick C.
Peasants in complex society.

(Basic anthropology units)
Bibliography: p. 74
1. Sociology, Rural.   2. Peasantry.   I. Title.
        HT421.G36   301.35   73–6554
                  ISBN: 0–03–091287–3

69694

Foreword

THE BASIC ANTHROPOLOGY UNITS

Basic Anthropology Units are designed to introduce students to essential topics in the contemporary study of man. In combination they have greater depth and scope than any single textbook. They may also be assigned selectively to cover topics relevant to the particular profile of a given course, or they may be utilized separately as authoritative guides to significant aspects of anthropology.

Many of the Basic Anthropology Units serve as the point of intellectual departure from which to draw on the Case Studies in Cultural Anthropology and Case Studies in Education and Culture. This integration is designed to enable instructors to utilize these easily available materials for their instructional purposes. The combination introduces flexibility and innovation in teaching and avoids the constraints imposed by the encyclopedic textbook. To this end, selected Case Studies have been annotated in each unit. Questions and exercises have also been provided as suggestive leads for instructors and students toward productive engagements with ideas and data in other sources as well as the Case Studies.

This series was planned over a period of several years by a number of anthropologists, some of whom are authors of the separate Basic Units. The completed series will include units representing all the basic sectors of contemporary anthropology, including archeology, biological anthropology, and linguistics, as well as the various subfields of social and cultural anthropology.

THE AUTHOR

Frederick C. Gamst is associate professor and associate of Lovett College at Rice University. He received his B.A. "with highest honors" from the University of California at Los Angeles and his Ph.D. from the University of California at Berkeley. He did fieldwork among peasants in Ethiopia during 1964 and 1965 and has taught courses at Rice on agrarian society and the problems of its modernization. In addition to research on peasants and agrarian society, Dr. Gamst has made extensive studies of railroaders in the United States in his development of what he calls "industrial and organizational ethnology" and is presently writing a book resulting from these studies. Dr. Gamst is a member of the committee guiding the Houston Inter-University African Studies Program. He plans to return to Ethiopia for further fieldwork among the peasantries of that country.

THIS UNIT

The study of peasants has undergone a modest efflorescence during the past decade, and for good reasons. It is possible to document many significant social, cultural, and psychological processes among them. They are strongholds of cultural persistence and yet are continuously influenced by and make adaptations to developments affecting the complex society of which they are a part. They express in their common features a reoccurring relationship between men, resources, power, and sociopolitical structure, as well as economic organization. They represent in their diversity the distinctive cultural traditions of the folk of various culture areas of the world. They are also at least marginal participants in the modern world of literate societies. Written records and historical sources add a new dimension to anthropological studies. Peasants are also interesting because they are part of a society more complex than their own could be by itself. The relationships of the peasant sector with the other sectors of a complex society confront the anthropologist with new and exciting problems and force him to deal with the small community in a regional or national context.

The study of peasants is also rewarding because there are so many of them. More than half of the world's population today can be said to be peasant and another 20 percent or more may be recently "post-peasant."

Particularly compelling is the argument presented by Fred Gamst in the last chapter of this unit, "The Future of Peasants in the Modernizing World." The peasant adaptation, as he suggests, may well be the one that survives. In any event it is clear that the modernization model presented by the United States with only 6 percent of the world's population but consuming over 40 percent of its goods is not a viable one for the rest of the world nor, in the long run, for the United States.

George and Louise Spindler
General Editors
STANFORD, CALIF.

Acknowledgments

I am in debt to a number of people who have helped me during the various stages in the development of this unit. Because the book was written as an introduction on the college level to the study of peasant society and culture, its development has benefited over the years from the questions and comments of my students, to whom I am grateful. Student assistance with the locating and retrieval of publications and other information from Rice University's Fondren Library was provided by Toni Moore, Lesley Wurth, and Ginna McClure. Sue Woodson typed the final draft of the manuscript, and William Fulton printed my photographs and produced the copy of the painting, *The Man with the Hoe.* My wife, Marilou, deserves special thanks for typing the preliminary drafts of the manuscript and for her critical commentary on and editing of the manuscript, not to mention her aid during my fieldwork among peasants in Ethiopia. George and Louise Spindler have provided their customary careful editing and constructive criticism for which I am grateful.

F. C. G.

Contents

BASIC ANTHROPOLOGY UNITS

GENERAL EDITORS
George and Louise Spindler
STANFORD UNIVERSITY

PEASANTS IN COMPLEX SOCIETY

O masters, lords and rulers in all lands,
How will the future reckon with this Man?
How answer his brute questions in that hour
When whirlwinds of rebellion shake all shores?
How will it be with kingdoms and with kings—
With those who shaped him to the thing he is—
When this dumb Terror shall rise to judge the world,
After the silence of the centuries?

—Edwin Markham, "The Man with the Hoe" (1899)

1
Introduction

Between one-half and two-thirds of today's world population of about 3.6 billion people may be considered peasants, and by far most of the human beings who have ever lived may be so considered. In the New World, peasantries exist today throughout Latin America. In the Old World, they are found in a broad central belt starting from the Atlantic nations—spanning the region from Scandinavia through Morocco—and extending across Europe, Northern Africa, Southwest Asia, Central Asia, the Indian subcontinent, and the Far East, terminating in Japan and Indonesia.

Activities of peasants have repeatedly dominated newspaper headlines during the twentieth century. These activities range from resistance movements of peasants in Russia, Yugoslavia, China, and Viet Nam during World War II, to more recent rebellions and revolutions—in large measure peasant in origin—in Indo-China, Algeria, China, Cuba, Yemen, Ethiopia, and Bangladesh. Because peasants overwhelm the earth with their numbers, the influences of their existence reverberate across the globe, even to the seemingly most secure of the world centers of affluence. Therefore, the subject of this book and its information are of immediate relevance to the understanding of the contemporary problems of man and are important to a full comprehension of his history.

THE ANTHROPOLOGICAL STUDY OF PEASANT CULTURE

Anthropological study of peasant culture goes at least as far back as the formal beginnings of the discipline in the mid-1800s. For example, Edward Tylor and Sir Henry Maine, two early ethnologists of the nineteenth century, used information from peasant, as well as tribal, life to formulate their ideas on culture. However, the interest of cultural anthropologists remained fixed for some time upon so-called primitive peoples, those on the tribal levels of organization. The study of peasants was not to be one of the central concerns of ethnology until the 1930s. Pioneering ethnologists who helped bring about this new concern by conducting fieldwork among peasants were Manuel Gamio (1922), Robert Redfield (1930), and Elsie Clews Parsons (1936).

Through the 1940s and 1950s, the interest of ethnologists in peasant culture gradually waxed. Today, more ethnologists study folk of the peasant and urban spheres of developing countries with agricultural civilizations than any other kind of people. This should not be surprising since we have already noted that most of the world's population consists of peasants, and the great numbers of these rural sedentary folk are increased by hundreds of millions of related urban folk of the preindustrial and industrializing cities of agricultural states. Thus, peasantries comprise much of the available subject matter for ethnological (and any other kind of social scientific) research. The Case Studies in Cultural Anthropology provide a good selection of examples of the results of such research. (An annotated list of Studies is provided at the end of this volume.) Much of the growth of the cultural anthropological theory of peasant culture and the bulk of the ethnographic data on it have been generated since 1960. Today's students of peasants may therefore be considered contemporary pioneers in social science.

American and Western European anthropologists were not the only scholars pioneering the study of peasants, and continuing these studies into the present. Related to the ethnological "school" in their subject matter are a number of other "schools" of study of peasants, of which we now mention two significant examples. Daniel Thorner tells us in his introduction to Alexander V. Chayanov's classic (originally published in the 1920s), *The Theory of Peasant Economy*: "Most of those who are today seeking to understand the economic behavior of the peasantry seem to be unaware that they are traversing much the same ground trod from the 1860's onward by several generations of Russian economists" (1966:xi). Chayanov's classic is an excellent introduction to this Russian social scientific literature. His book concerns family-oriented peasant economics, in which wage labor is absent. This kind of economics, according to Chayanov, requires a theory different from formal orthodox economics. We should also note a broad international "school" of regional European studies largely falling outside the rubric of the social sciences and into that of the humanities. This school is customarily labeled *Volkskunde* (folklore or study of folk) and is opposed to *Völkerkunde* (ethnology). For further information on and an excellent example of the study of folk (peasants, in this use) see Fél and Hofer (1969) and also the issue of the *East European Quarterly* (1970) devoted to this subject.

Ethnological study of peasant culture has three foci. First, ethnologists usually conduct field research in a peasant community for a minimum period of one year. Information is gathered primarily through participant observation and informal interviewing, especially of key-informants, and secondarily through any or all of the following: censuses, structured interview schedules and questionnaires, collection of genealogies, recording of life histories, and projective psychological tests. It is from the substantive data derived in large part from the community study that the ethnologist works inductively to hypothesize on the other two foci: the peasant subculture of which the community is a unit and, more infrequently, the civilization of which the peasantry constitutes the largest component.

Additionally, an ethnologist may use the comparative method to arrive at generalizations on peasantries, or any other cultural type. Here, empirical data from many field studies are compared to arrive at what is common to all. Further information on the development and organization of peasant communities and their agrarian states comes from the excavation and analysis of archeological data. Anthropologists sometimes combine information from two of the fields of their discipline and thereby use ethnological and archeological data to generalize on peasantries. For further study of the techniques and procedures of ethnological fieldwork see Pelto

1970 and Spindler 1970 and also the information and bibliographies contained in the following titles in the Studies in Anthropological Method series: Beattie (1965); Collier (1967); Henry and Saberwal (1969); Hsu (1969); Langness (1965); and Williams (1967).

THE PEASANT IN COMPLEX SOCIETY AND THE STATE

Peasants and peasant cultures cannot be understood apart from the complex society, and the state, of which they are a part. The political organization of any complex society is that of one or more states. The economic base of these states ranges from agricultural to industrial. We turn first to a consideration of complex society and then to the state and its relation to peasants.

Complex Society   No strict definition of complex society exists in anthropology despite the prevalence of the term. Indeed, it is rarely, if ever, defined at all in writings on the subject. In this unit when we speak of complex society we mean the social organizational aspect of a developmental level of culture known as civilization, a concept about which considerable agreement exists among anthropologists. Complex societies and their peasantries may be viewed as extending along a developmental continuum of modernization from a polar type of agricultural civilization to another polar type of industrial urban civilization. When we speak of traditional or classic peasants, or other cultural types, we merely refer to a type removed from industrial urban conditions, hence, in the case of peasants, one at or near the agrarian pole of the continuum. In this unit when we refer to "peasant society," and to its larger agrarian social order, we refer in general to types anywhere along this continuum of development, except at or near the point of full industrial urbanism, where peasants and agrarian society no longer exist. At times we will specifically restrict our discussion to a particular segment of the continuum, for example, "classic peasants" or "postpeasants."

At this point we should note that the various aspects of sociocultural reality, which scholars and others may discuss, exist in many continua of variation and not in absolutely or universally delimited categories or boxes. However, it is difficult to grasp and to deal with an entire continuum, whether its analysis is of a scientific or a "man-on-the-street" kind. Thus, men arbitrarily delimit and invariably label a number of partially contrastive segments of a continuum under consideration. Following a custom in Western science, we refer to polar (extreme) ends of certain continua during our examination of peasants. For purposes of scientific analysis, it is sometimes useful to identify not two but several or even many categories along a continuum. Whether an analytic framework has two or many categories, it does not become invalid with the ethnographic identification of cases transitional to or bordering the working categories of the analysis. For example, the fact that the indigenous pre-Columbian civilizations and peasantries of the New World do not entirely fall within the constructs used here, does not mean our presentation is invalid.

Our explanatory use of the traditional-agrarian polar type does not, of course, mean that before contact with industrialism all agrarian societies are alike in their economic and political complexity. On the contrary, a comparison of seventeenth-century China, France, Russia, Ethiopia, Persia, and Morocco shows the great diversity of content and range of organizational complexity of agricultural civilization. They all share a difference of kind, however, from the organizational complexity and energy-harnessing capacity of industrial civilization.

Before discussing the importance of the state for the existence of peasantries, we outline the evolution of complex society, and its different kinds of states, from less complex forms of society. Culture, including that of peasants who are so often said to be changeless, constantly changes. Certain cultures and subcultures, and certain aspects or subsystems of these, change at different rates than others. The term used to encompass all of cultural change is cultural evolution, a continuous development each stage of which unfolds from a previous stage. Cultural evolution may be considered as specific, the sequential adaptive changes of a particular or specific culture to its environment, and as general, the over-all change of culture considered in its panhuman, or generic, sense (see Sahlins and Service 1960: 12–44). Evolutionary change usually leads to increasing complexity and diversity of sociocultural organization and function with the harnessing of increasingly greater amounts of energy as the principle function (cf. White 1949, 1959; *Scientific American* 1971). A basic differentiator of peasant-agrarian society, and those of lower technological levels, from industrial society is the very small amounts of energy harnessed per capita by the former as opposed to the very large amounts harnessed by the developed forms of the latter.

Culture has evolved generally through what may be thought of as a number of levels of cultural integration centered upon technology and its means for harnessing and utilizing energy. For the levels below that of the state, this evolution may be explained as developing from egalitarian societies into hierarchical societies (cf. Service 1971:157). With the conclusion of this subsection, for the sake of brevity and for want of a more felicitous term, we shall include both of these levels under the general rubric of "tribal" society and culture. From the level of hierarchical societies, development continues into what we shall discuss in this book as the incipient state, then into the (fully developed) agrarian state of complex society, and then into the industrial state of complex society. The specific evolution of most cultures has not yet fully reached the industrial level, as we shall see, and many of the world's states are still largely supported by direct and indirect taxes upon peasants and are therefore largely agrarian. Many cultures today are largely on the hierarchical level, and a few are still on the egalitarian level.

Specific evolution of particular cultures does not take place independently. On the contrary, the evolution of cultures is interwoven with diffusion between cultures, that is, transmission of elements of cultures across distances (and hence over time), ranging from local to global. Thus, because of the diffusion of patterns of industrial culture to contemporary tribalists, these peoples need not evolve through an intermediate level of agrarian states in order to reach an industrial level of cultural integration. Accordingly, most of the world's tribal societies, as in sub-Saharan Africa, are beginning modernization toward an industrial level within the framework of only recently emerged modernizing postcolonial states. (Compare, however, Derman 1972 for views, in part, opposed to our contention.) This new type of state has a government approximating the kind found in industrial states and has the beginnings of an industrial urban infrastructure.

The State   Rather than follow the lead of the many works that deal with the consequences of the state without saying what is meant by "the state," we shall discuss this concept, but not without some hesitancy. Definitions of the state are varied and ambiguous and often do not go beyond an explanation of its organization into a necessary explanation of its political process.

To facilitate understanding of this concept, we begin with the premise that every culture has its political aspect, or subsystem. It *openly* functions to guide some part of behavior toward group interests and maintenance. Other subsystems of culture may have political functions, but such guiding of behavior by these subsystems is latent, not readily apparent to the carriers of the culture. A stateless society, then, has a political organization. However, it has no *centralized* and *formal* political institutions, that is, those covering all of the society and set apart from others in the society. In stateless societies, political functions of institutions are open but are secondary to, or at least connected to, other functions such as kinship, association, or religion.

We view the state as a particular stage in the evolution of political organization, one evolved from informally institutionalized politics in tribal societies. The state's underlying organization is that of a centralized, territorially related, formal political institution. The territorial base of a state may be that of a city, thus a city-state, or it may encompass all or part of a culture (an ethnic group), thus a nation-state. Many ethnic groups may be encompassed by a state, thus a supernational state such as India or the Soviet Union.

The state has a publicly acknowledged (thereby legitimate) and exclusive control over the use of social power to direct, to the point of coercion if necessary, the activities of its inhabitants, within certain limits prescribed by law. This prerogative of the state to direct activities is often delegated in part and is never completely exercised. The legitimate use of social power to direct the action of others is known as authority, and the state has a monopoly on authority. In all, we may view the state as a sovereign organization of political institutions, the governing power of which is recognized and conformed to by the population of the territory over which it has jurisdiction.

The basic power of the state, then, is in its claim to a monopoly over the use of violent physical force to achieve political goals. This claim includes maintaining its independence from other states through warfare and maintaining internal order through law enforcement, including at times the legal killing or other punishment of violators of the law. Put another way, the basic power of the state is ultimately derived from a weapon. Constant recourse to naked force by a state, however, would remove from the realm of legitimacy its use of social power. Thus other means of control of behavior must be intertwined with and at times veil the fundamental power of the state. A "velvet glove" must be used to clothe the "mailed fist" which the state ultimately can always use. Diplomacy and ideological appeals are also employed by the state as a means of maintaining social harmony and security, and this is the case more frequently than is the use of force. For example, more often than the state's use of physical force, negotiations are begun with another state, and the peasant is exhorted to honor government and church and to protect the sacred fatherland. Of course, the state's potential for the use of force always supports the use of diplomacy and the appeal to ideology; peasants who do not volunteer are conscripted to defend the holy fatherland.

As part of its monopoly on authority, the governmental agents of the state administer its law. We may consider state law as a system of regulations of conduct made by recognized administrators, but often originating in customary rules for conduct. Laws are enacted to enforce modes of justice, often varying according to a person's status, and to prescribe some of the differing rights and obligations of inhabitants of a state. Modes of justice are interrelated with the state's maintenance of a particular hierarchy of social stratification, giving its inhabitants differing access to wealth and power. The status of the peasant ranks very low in any state hierarchy, and he normally has little access to wealth and power.

We now expand upon our distinction between the three stages on the evolutionary continuum of the development of the state in order to show the relation of peasant society to its larger social order. Emerging from tribalism, an incipient state is ethnically homogeneous and has a political organization whose sovereignty is less fully consolidated than that of the agrarian civilized state. In recent times, with changes in economy from an agrarian to an industrial orientation and with increased political centralization, we may speak of the industrial state. Prehistoric and more recent incipient states, such as those of East Africa and some of those of West Africa, usually have a horticultural economic basis (a moderately intensive production of crops with hand tools), but may sometimes have a pastoral basis. The agrarian civilized state usually has an economic basis of intensive agriculture. Increasingly more efficient and productive technologies do not invariably produce incipient and then, eventually, civilized states. These technologies may be viewed as a necessary but not sufficient basis for the support of state organizations.

In the course of this unit we shall refer to "agrarian" societies and states as a shorthand form for the more descriptive but cumbersome modifier "agrarian civilized." The political element we are labeling "civilized" emerged during the course of cultural evolution as the governing elite and the governed commoners of the agriculturally based state became markedly socially differentiated from each other and as both government and this differentiation became reinforced by writing. This form of sociopolitical organization distinguishes peasant cultivators and other peasant producers from cultivators and other producers of the tribe and the incipient state.

Peasants may be viewed as one of three kinds of *folk*, illiterate and nearly powerless commoners originating with and found within the social organization of the civilized state. The other two are *townsmen*, living in preindustrial urban centers, and *pastoralists*, those herders who are controlled to some extent by a civilized state. The state's formal political institutions, controlled by an elite, are the means of effective subordination of commoners. Additional informal political patterns reinforce these formal institutions.

In an agrarian state there are territorial zones in which the strength of state authority varies. An inner zone of strong authority grades into a middle zone of lesser authority, often in mountainous areas and in more distant plains. An outer, borderland zone of little, nominal, or no state authority lies beyond the middle zone. The respective areas of these three zones fluctuate over the years with changes in the political and economic strength of a state. The inner and middle zones may be characterized in accordance with the writing of Carlton Coon (1958:263–64) as land of state order (Arabic: *Bled el-Makhzen*) and the border zone as land of insolence—in regard to state authority—(*Bled es-Siba*).

Before beginning the following chapter we should note that our use of the word "civilization" should not evoke any prejudicial connotations of innate racial or cultural superiority or inferiority. The word is used to denote in a concise way certain traits, according to largely shared conventions in social science. These conventions include a developed state organization and system of writing as well as other elements, elaborated upon in Chapter 2.

2
Agrarian Society

We now turn to the cultural evolutionary background of agricultural civilization, or agrarian society, and then to its continuing transformation into industrial urban civilizaton. We shall also examine the organization of the agrarian form of complex society, which originated with and today encompasses the world's peasants.

THE EVOLUTION OF PEASANTRIES IN AGRICULTURAL CIVILIZATION

For millions of years men, and hominids ancestral to men, were foragers, that is, hunters of animals and gatherers of plants, and were usually seminomadic. Foraging uses technological means energized by human muscle power alone. Quite recently—around 10,000 B.C., the end of the Pleistocene epoch of the earth's geological evolution—the cultural evolution of man reached a threshold which allowed the beginning of what has been termed a "revolutionary" transformation of his cultural development. This development centers upon man's increased cultural control of energy, which he uses to adapt to environment and to maintain and increase standards of living. The passing of this threshold by certain cultures resulted in their experiencing a period of several millennia of a marked and ever excellerating rate of specific cultural evolution. The revolutionary transformation in cultural integration was from the lifeway of foraging to one of sedentary husbandry of domesticated plants and animals, which provided greater energy resources for the evolution of culture. This transformation is called the Neolithic, or Agricultural, Revolution.

In terms of the energy theory of cultural evolution, as developed by Leslie A. White (1949, 1959), increasing amounts of energy harnessed and utilized through Neolithic technological development supported increasing societal evolution. By societal evolution is meant increasing complexity of social organization and differentiation, or specialization, of its functions. Thus, as Neolithic techniques of husbandry developed and increased in productivity, increasing numbers of men were freed from their primordial labor of food production, allowing them to enter an increasing diversity of other occupations including those of administration, crafts, and the military. By the eighth millennium B.C. in southwestern Asia, perhaps almost as early in Mesoamerica, and around the same time in southeastern Asia, the Neolithic Revolution was beginning. (For additional information on the Neolithic Revolution see Cole 1970.)

Secondary to the "revolutionary" energy-harnessing technologies of plant and animal domestication were those of potting, spinning, weaving, grinding of stone tools to size and shape, and the engineering and building of large structures of various kinds. These technological changes and interrelated changes in other aspects of culture, including kinship, economics, politics, and religion, freed man from the checks and balances of what may be viewed as a largely "natural" and "predatory" cultural ecology and substituted those of an increasingly environment-manipulating cultural ecology. In this new ecology, man, through his extraorganic culture, changes the geographical environment to which he adapts. In short, as a result of the cultural breakthrough of the Neolithic Revolution, man increasingly adapted to the geographical environment by modifying it to meet his needs.

After a few millennia of evolution from a Neolithic basis, some cultures in certain parts of the world entered a second evolutionary threshold, often called the Urban Revolution, but perhaps more appropriately named the Civilizing Revolution. The Neolithic Revolution primarily concerns changes in technology and economics, and secondarily those of sociopolitical organization. The Civilizing Revolution primarily concerns changes in sociopolitical organization, which developed from the earlier change to life styles related to agricultural harnessing of plant and animal energy.

Peasantries, and the agricultural civilizations of which they are a vital part, first emerged upon the earth in the river valleys of Mesopotamia and in western Iran in conjunction with the beginnings of urbanism and writing. They originated during the fourth millennium B.C. (See R. M. Adams 1966 for a stimulating analysis of the social organizational evolution of early civilization, or urban society.) From this time on we may speak of what has been called the "peasantizing" of a large part of the earth's population and area. The highly successful adaptations of agricultural civilization, including peasant culture, soon diffused from southwestern Asia to the Nile Valley of Egypt, and the Indus Valley of India. During the second millenium B.C., the adaptations evolved in the Yellow River Valley of China, possibly as a result of stimulation from further west. The region of Old World agricultural civilization is sometimes referred to as the ecumene, or oikoumene. By the end of the first millenium B.C., the ecumene had expanded into virtually all of the broad central belt of Eurasia and northern Africa.

Agricultural civilization evolved, apparently independently, during the second millennnium B.C. in the Mesoamerican and Central Andean regions of the New World. This evolution during any point in time was not entirely emerged from its Neolithic antecedents and was thus not at the same level of sociopolitical complexity and efficiency and technological and economic development as it was in the Old World. This was in part because of the lack of a fully developed system of writing used for purposes of governmental administration and keeping of commercial records. We might best characterize the New World civilizations and their peasantries as transitional to more fully developed stages, and as organized into advanced forms of the incipient state. Apropos of this statement, we cite William McNeill's monumental culture history, *The Rise of the West.* "In general, the level of these American civilizations in 600 A.D. was roughly comparable to that of the ancient river valley civilizations of Mesopotamia, Egypt, and the Indus about 3000 B.C. . . . This places the rise of American civilizations more than 3500 years behind comparable evolution in the Old World. . . ." (1963:416). During the six-teenth century A.D., the agrarian state of Spain easily conquered the New World civilizations and brought them within the thereby expanded confines of the Old World ecumene. This resulted in the acculturation of the populations of the New World civilizations, toward Spanish-Mediterranean culture, and the demise of their states. The concept of peasantry, according to the definition to be developed in the following pages, is used more fittingly in the ecumene, including its recent expansion into the New World, than in the parallel evolutionary beginnings of peasantry in the Andean and Mesoamerican civilizations not yet fully emerged from a Neolithic basis.

After its essentially full development in its so-called Copper and Iron Ages, agricultural civilization did not greatly change until the beginnings of its recent (eighteenth century A.D.) transformation, which has not occurred in all parts of the agrarian world. The transformation was into a revolutionary new cultural integration, activated by the vastly increased amounts of energy available to man from his industrial harnessing of fossil fuels such as coal.

THE TRANSFORMATION OF AGRARIAN SOCIETY

Until very recently, the ecumene of agricultural states, supported by the human labor and draft animals used in peasant production of food stuffs, fibers, and animal feeds, covered all of the areas of the earth not still populated by people on the tribal levels of cultural evolution. The millennia-old agrarian way of life began its transformation first in Britain, where the Industrial Revolution was underway during the mid-1700s, and then in northwestern Europe and the United States during the 1800s. This beginning of the industrialization of the ecumene, and its consequent domination by the West, was at a time when the agrarian ecumene was still expanding throughout Latin America under the aegis of Iberian civilization and across Siberia under the Russians.

The Industrial Revolution (or equally apt, the Fossil Fuel Revolution) was an outgrowth of antecedent cultural developments of later agricultural civilization, especially those of science and of mercantilistic commerce and navigation. The last two mercantile developments resulted in the beginnings of the monetized global market, through which the growth of industrialism could be nourished. We may say that during the Industrial Revolution, the general cultural evolution of man passed another threshold into a new level of cultural integration. This threshold was based upon the ever increasing multiplication and rationalization of human productivity through the use of machines energized by fossil fuels. The crossing of this technological threshold by, what were as a consequence, industrializing states led to great rates of change in the specific cultural evolution within these states. This change would soon transform the world's peasantries (and other pre-industrial peoples), because industrialism and its concomitants diffused during the nineteenth and twentieth centuries from Western Europe and the United States to the world's agrarian states, incipient states, and tribal areas. Today the global ecumene is industrialized in some regions and is in various stages of industrialization in the other regions.

The modernized world is customarily labeled as being industrial urban, that is, all industrial states are highly urbanized and all industrializing states are accelerating in the growth of their urban populations. The urban half of this label refers to two phenomena. One phenomenon is the growth, supported by industry, of supersized cities (such as New York) with populations in the millions. Related to this growth is the burgeoning sprawl of cities along arteries of transportation into a number of multicentered urban continuua, or megalopoli, such as those of Boston-New York-Washington and Los Angeles-San Diego. A measure of the degree of a state's modernization is the percentage of its population residing in urban areas. The highly modernized United States, for example, by 1970 had approximately sixty percent of its 200 million people concentrated in somewhat over 200 urbanized areas comprising only one percent of its territory. According to some definitions of the Bureau of the Census, half of the remaining forty percent of the population may also be classified as urban, that is, living in communities of 2500 or more. The constantly shrinking farm population of the United States accounted for less than one-quarter of the remaining (or rural) twenty percent, or only 4.7 percent of the total population!

The other phenomenon is the assimilation of rural culture into a mass urban culture either of a national state or of an ethnic territory (such as the Tamil region of India) of a supernational state. In the highly modernized countries—again, for example, the United States—urban culture diffuses to ensnare and transform the lifestyle of the most remote of rural communities through the media of relatively uniform public education, industrialized transportation and communication (such as motor vehicles, radio, and popular publications), and marketing of standardized products.

As agricultural civilizations across the globe modernize into industrial urban civilizations, their peasants become what may be called *postpeasants*, having only some of the attributes of peasants discussed in the following section. In industrializing states postpeasants become involved in an increasingly more capital-intensive and less labor-intensive cultivation which transforms those that remain on the land into one of two major types of *modern agriculturalists: farmers* or *farming collectivists.*

Farmers are agricultural entrepreneurs who control land, labor, and capital for the production of plants and animals sold into a monetized and globally inter-related market which to some extent determines prices of farm production. (Government usually enters this market to stabilize fluctuations in price.) *Farm laborers* control either their own labor alone or else their labor and their own machinery, such as trucks or harvesting equipment, and sell their services to farmers in what is largely a market economy. Farming collectivists are of at least two major subtypes approximating those agriculturalists characteristic of the Soviet Union. "Soviet agriculture has two main forms, the *kolkhoz,* which in theory is owned and controlled by the membership, and the *sovkhoz,* owned and controlled by the central government, which takes all profits and assumes all risks" (Dunn and Dunn 1967:39). Farming collectivists usually produce in relation to a price structure which is adjusted more by an economic system of state collection and redistribution than by markets (for more information on these matters see Chapter 4, Economics of Exchange in Peasant Society). Actually the cultivators of the Soviet Union are not as yet fully emerged from peasantry (see Dunn and Dunn 1967) as farming collectivists, and may thus be considered in an advanced stage of transition into becoming a type of modern agriculturalist.

The pace of modernization of agrarian states has been very uneven and thus today we find populations of peasants at all of the developmental intervals between the remaining classic peasants, as in Ethiopia, and the postpeasants transforming into farmers (cf. Spindler 1973) and farming collectivists (cf. Dunn and Dunn 1967), as in parts of northwestern and eastern Europe.

THE ORGANIZATION OF AGRICULTURAL CIVILIZATION AND ITS PEASANT SECTOR

The Salient Factors in Agrarian Organization   In this unit an attempt is made not only to depict peasant culture, and society, but also to examine its complex civilizational setting, a portrayal necessary for a true understanding of peasants. Customary ethnological field studies of peasants are community-oriented and are therefore useful for looking at local aspects of lifeways of peasants; however, these frequently omit or slight extracommunity aspects. A true holistic approach, that is, comprehending interrelations between all parts of culture, must be grounded in a study of a peasant community *and* its relations to the complex society of which it is but a part, and in which so much action is taken affecting the peasant way.

Peasants as a cultural type constitute a broad category with certain cultural common denominators. Thus many crosscultural regularities of structure and of setting exist between the hundreds of peasantries upon the face of the earth. Surrounding this universalness is a considerable range of characteristics not entirely shared by all peasantries. Therefore, in speaking of peasants as a cultural type, we should not become caught up in argument over whether or not a particular group accords entirely with a general model of peasantries. Within a framework of peasant universals, cultural anthropological definitions of peasants vary, but most focus upon certain central themes. Several of these are combined here to create a working definition of peasant culture as a framework for the rest of the unit.

In general, a peasantry may be thought of as constituting a subsystem (or sector) of an agrarian society, which may be partly or largely located along the developmental continuum into the stage of industrial society. An agrarian civilization, and its peasants, may be discussed in one of two intertwined ways, categorically in terms of description of the basic content of its cultural inventory, and structurally in terms of systemic relationships between its various sociocultural elements. We shall retain the intertwining of both of these ways in our discussion of peasants.

Two attributes (which may be considered both structurally and categorically) of agricultural civilization are particularly significant and are central to our discussion of peasants. The first is a state society which has a dual organization, that is, a superordinate sector of the elite and one or more subordinate sectors of commoners. The dual society is socially stratified. The second is a developed system of writing. Also significant is the presence of all or most of the following: agriculture—cultivation with plow and draft animals or else intensive cultivation (usually irrigated) with hand tools; great proliferation of statuses that have full-time craft and other occupational specializations; political transformation of some of the agricultural production into monumental architecture; a moderately developed marketing system; urban centers; and long distance trade. To illustrate briefly what we have said about the intertwining of categorical and structural considerations, "long distance trade" is not merely listed here as part of a description of categories of cultural inventory. By its very existence this category refers to systemic social relationships, in this case, a symbiotic relationship between different geographical regions engaged in trade, including the states of these regions. The structural significance of the other categories are discussed in the rest of this section and throughout the remainder of this unit.

In addition to those just mentioned for the encompassing agrarian society, categorical and structural considerations of a peasantry include the following. Basic is small-scale, rural agricultural and sometimes craft production, using preindustrial equipment and techniques on a subsistence or near subsistence level. The family is the central social unit of production, and when the peasants are agriculturalists—as they are most often—the family is the land-using unit. Cultivating peasants may be considered as "tied to the land." However, holding of land, although common, is not necessary for inclusion of subordinated cultivators under the rubric of peasantry. Because the peasant family is not entirely self-sufficient, it usually sells some part of its production in a market system of exchange and purchases certain essential goods there. It also surrenders some part of its production to members of an elite, because of their superior claim to this production, a claim based upon authority received from the state.

Expanding upon our two common denominators of agricultural civilization and its peasant sector, we note that by "dual" we mean the society is divided into a small controlling group of exploitative elite (aristocrats) and a very large supporting group of commoners, consisting mostly of peasants. As we shall see, the basic societal cleavage between elite administrators and commoner producers is structurally more significant than the gradations of rank within the two societal halves. By "stratified" we mean the social positions, or statuses, of the two halves of society are ranked together from high, where few statuses exist, to low, where statuses of the vast majority are found at or near the base of the social pyramid.

Related to social stratification is a complex division of labor with great diversity of occupational statuses. We especially find in urban, and at times in rural settings, the statuses of higher secular administrators of government, higher priests (who are sometimes government administrators), supportive lower administrators and priests, scribes, accountants, engineers, nonpeasant craftsmen, merchants, nonagricultural laborers, soldiers, servants, beggars, entertainers, and slaves. In rural settings, we find the statuses of peasants and pastoralists. Statuses tend to be ascribed, or fixed by birth, rather than achieved by individual effort, as is more the case within industrial states.

Central to the concept of dual social organization of the agrarian state is the exercise of social power by the members of the elite part of this organization in what becomes a legitimate control of nonelites. Especially important here is the elites' superior claim to and taking of part of the production of the masses of peasants and sometimes of the small number of pastoralists. The exercising of this claim provides not only for the maintenance of the elite, but also for that of the state. Payments to a member of this elite because of his superior claim may be in money, goods, and labor. The definition of the peasant by the existence of such an elite's claim to a part of his production because of the latter's superior power, or jurisdiction, was developed by the anthropologist Eric Wolf (1966:3–4, 9–10, 50–59). Concerning these payments, which he labels as "rent," Wolf says:

> I . . . regard rent not merely as an economic payment for the use of land, but as a payment made by virtue of relations of power that in the case of peasants, but not in the case of primitives [tribalists], are guaranteed by the state (1972:411).

Our second common denominator of agricultural civilization is a developed system of writing. The elite as a group are literate, whereas peasants and other commoners are illiterate, unable to read and write in a social system containing literacy. This provides a further refinement of our analytic filter with which we distinguish peasants from (preliterate) tribal peoples, for writing further differentiates and fixes the dual social organization of the state. Members of the elite refer to bodies of writing for legal and supernatural support of their claim to power, as in the legal codes proclaiming among other things that the monarch is "king by grace of God." The elite also use writing as an administrative tool to control peasants and to enforce their superior claim to part of peasant production.

Related to and reinforcing the definition of peasants by their inclusion in the subordinate half of a dual social organization is the notion of peasant ways of life as part of what has been called a bifurcated Tradition, or a culture consisting of two major divisions, in which writing structures social relations. In this view, developed by historian Ralph Turner (1941:1:269–270, 315–323) and refined by anthropologist Robert Redfield (1955a:16–27) a lifeway of a peasantry is a Little Tradition, that is, a "low" subculture or illiterate "folk" manifestation of a culture. This culture also has a lifeway of an elite or a Great Tradition, that is, an elaborate "high" subculture based upon literacy. In short, writing makes more absolute the contrast between elite and peasant society and culture, in addition to making more administratively efficient the superior claim of the elite to part of peasant production. Of course, not all power wielding members of the elite sector of agrarian society have been individually literate. Many nobles of high rank could no more read and write than they could lead their men in battle. The important thing is that the elite collectively controlled literacy, and the often powerless scribes and accountants kept the records.[1]

During modernization of agrarian societies a Mass Tradition gradually replaces most of the classic bifurcated Tradition. The Mass Tradition is a modern popular urban culture which in time permeates the remotest of rural settings and assimilates the Little Traditions. Many traces of the Little Tradition remain in rural areas even during advanced stages of modernization (cf. Spindler 1973:51–85). Many elements of the agrarian Great Tradition also remain as in contemporary Europe, among the new and old elites, who also share the popular urban culture with the lower and middle classes.

Agrarian Social Sectors and Agrarian Part Societies   Continuing the discussion

---

[1] For further information on the social consequences of writing in agrarian society and on the concept of bifurcation of civilized Tradition see Anderson 1971a:35–42; Childe 1951: 144–152; Fallers 1961; Foster 1953; Goody 1968; Goody and Watt 1963; Marriott 1955; Redfield 1947:296–297; 1953a:228; 1953b:36–37, 42–43; 1955a; Sjoberg 1960:8–11, 32–34, 286–318; and Weingrod 1969.

| E L I T E |||
GREAT TRADITION		
N o b i l i t y	C l e r g y	G e n t r y

C O M M O N E R S			
N O N F O L K GREAT OR LITTLE TRADITION	**F O L K** LITTLE TRADITION		
B u r g h e r s	P e a s a n t s	T o w n s m e n	P a s t o r a l i s t s

Relationships between sectors of the dual social organization of the agrarian state.

of agricultural civilization, we turn to the description of it developed by the anthropologist Alfred Kroeber (1947:323; 1948:284; and cf. also Redfield 1940: xiv–xv). In Kroeber's terms, what we have called a dually organized agrarian state may alternatively be considered structurally as consisting of several *part societies with part cultures*—those of urbanites, those of (rural) peasants, and where subjugated by the state, those of (rural) pastoralists. Each part society has a number of social structures which are made complete by those in the other parts of the agrarian society.

In the analysis of peasants and agricultural civilization, we have found it worthwhile to modify Kroeber's model and to think instead in terms of social sectors of the dual components of the agrarian state. In our view, the state may be considered as having at least two but usually more sectors. It ordinarily consists of an elite sector and several commoner sectors. Elite of various kinds comprise the only sector of the elite component of the dual state organization. The commoner component of this organization has three folk sectors—peasants, pastoralists, and townsmen—and, at times, one nonfolk commoner sector of burghers. Each of the sectors is dependent upon the others for its maintenance. Some agrarian states have no pastoral sector and a few, lacking urbanism, have no townsman sector.

The elite sector cuts across the "part societies," as conceived by Kroeber. We make this point since many users of the concept of the peasant-urban dichotomy sometimes write as if they equate the elite with urbanites, and this is not ethnographically so, as we shall now explain. (Also, peasants who have recently migrated and some nonpeasant folk, in many ways similar to peasants, live in urban centers. Peasants newly arrived in town commonly maintain ties with rural kinsmen and friends for a couple of generations.) Many members of the elite sector reside in preindustrial urban centers. Some usually reside in the countryside, and in the case of certain agrarian states all dwell rurally (cf. Gamst 1970). All elite reside in the midst of folk. The kind of residence and composition of any particular civilization are determined by its specific evolution.

A townsman plowing his fields on the edge of Gondar Town, Ethiopia, with equipment and in a manner exactly the same as that of the peasants in the surrounding countryside. Many of the world's townsmen are also full- or part-time cultivators.

In the elite organization, urban or rural, the central roles focus upon administration of authority. The paramount ruler or rulers among the elite usually dwell in cities. They exercise a great amount ·of power, limited by tendencies on the part of the subordinate elite toward autonomy and by the encroaching power of other states. Other limitations are generated by the latent collective power of the sectors of commoners. The elite sector may be organized into separate secular and clerical (religious) hierarchies, but sometimes the two kinds of elite are merged. At times, the secular elite consists of nobility and a subordinate nonnoble gentry, as in agrarian England. More rarely, the gentry may largely replace the nobility as the power-wielding elite, as in Imperial China.

Agrarian societies frequently have another, smaller, sector of rural producers besides the sedentary peasant. Some rural producers may instead constitute a sector of pastoralists (cf. Redfield 1956:18). As with pastoralists of the Islamic Arabian civilization, the herdsmen may have a Little Tradition similar to that of nearby peasants. The pastoral Little Tradition is adapted to a more nomadic way of life, often found in outlying lands of marginal productivity not firmly controlled by the state. Herders of regions outside of the civilized ecumene, for example the Masai of eastern Africa or the Tongus of Siberia, have no Little Tradition (Gamst 1970: 389). The pastoral sector is gradated from those herders rather strictly subordinated to a state to tribal herders just coming under the jurisdiction of the elite. The degree of subordination varies with the power of the state.

The townsmen are illiterate and almost powerless, like the other folk, but reside instead in a preindustrial urban setting which they share with many elite and others. Townsmen may have any of the occupations outside of those of the elite and those of their retainers. Their occupations at times even include cultivation of plots of land just outside of town.

The peasant sector of an agrarian state may also grade away from true peasants (with a strict political subordination to the elite of a state and with a Little Tradition version of an elite's Great Tradition) to tribal cultivators just coming into the fold of civilization. Those in a tribalist-peasant transitional stage have varying extents of less-than-strict subordinations. They also may have varying extents of a "Secondary Little Tradition," a distinct former tribal culture, such as that of the Qemant division of the Agaw of Ethiopia, partially acculturated to a bifurcated Tradition of a civilization, such as that of Amhara elite and folk in Ethiopia (cf. Gamst 1970:374–375). Or else, they may have a peripheral variant of a Secondary Little Tradition belonging to a division of their own ethnic group, already well along the road to peasantry. Examples of this are found among the more tribal Berbers and Agaw of northern Africa. Tribesmen in transition to peasants are often mountaineers of "the land of insolence," as among some Atlas Berbers, Zagros Kurds, Ethiopian Highland Agaw, Hindu Kush Pathans, and "hill" tribes of India. Groups of settled tribal cultivators may be alternatively embraced and released by the confines of the state according to the waxing and waning of state power. Today, few of these transitional tribalist-peasants remain near the autonomous tribal end of the continuum to peasantry, although some Berbers and Kurds are still nowhere near a full integration into their modernizing agrarian states.

At times, certain townsmen acquire wealth and power not expressly, or at least not willingly, delegated to them by the elite. This acquisition is usually derived through commerce, preindustrial manufacturing, mining, and, sometimes, middle or high military rank. In such instances we may find the emergence of a fourth social sector of commoners, who, in this case, are not folk. We shall call them *burghers*, after the relatively large and successful kind of nonfolk commoners found in the urban centers of the European agricultural states beginning around 1000 A.D. As a group, burghers are often literate, and hence do not experience the near powerlessness of folk and the subsequent abject poverty. Burghers, townsmen, and certain members of the elite may be collectively called *urbanites.*

The literate subcultures of burghers of agrarian Europe were necessary for the cultural evolutionary development known as the Industrial Revolution. This, we have noted, began in the northwest of this region during the 1700s, where the roots of the Revolution are found in part in burgher commercialism and struggles against the elite for some degree of political autonomy. During the advanced stages of this commercialism, in the 1600s, came the entry of certain wealthy burghers into the elite half of societal organization. Eventually, with the beginnings of the flowering of the industrial state in Europe, a *new elite*—"captains" of industry, commerce, and the military and also high-ranking government administrators, all of whom are usually descendants of certain burghers—begins to replace the old, agrarian elite to become the, sometimes invisible, wielders of political power. However, during recent decades, many developing states have an oligarchic and quasimilitary new elite, which is sometimes a partial outgrowth of the old elite, is often quite visible, and is politically allied to developed nations.

A few burghers may become members of the new elite of the upper class of industrial society; however, most burghers of developing countries eventually become members of an ever growing industrial urban middle class. In industrial society, the structure of the traditional dual organization and the social boundary around the elite component softens and becomes hazy through time. This especially happens as universal free education supported by the state enters the scene, as more inhabitants of a state fully enter a monetized national market economy, and as the modern Mass Tradition begins to replace the Great and Little Traditions.

During this modernizing transformation of the agrarian state, an industrial and a farming proletarian sector emerges. These proletarians are urban and rural manual laborers without property and who thus control no capital within an industrializing or industrialized state. Such proletarians may come from the ranks of townsmen and from rural folk who have migrated to the cities. They may also be rurally situated producers of foodstuffs, fibers, and crafts who either lose their rights to the means of production (for example, land) or lose their traditional niche in the economy during the time of industrialization. With advanced industrialization, as in the West, proletarians of these kinds develop into a relatively affluent "blue-collar" class. During the period of industrialization, folk of all three kinds endure and occupy the base of the socioeconomic pyramid alongside this new proletarian addition to the lower class. The peasants are especially enduring and tenacious in their hold upon the land and so are the postpeasants descended from them. The phenomenon of "peasant lag," that is, peasants remaining in a state with industrial urban centers, and perhaps with some farmers or farming collectivists, is fostered by public and private policies of investment in manufacturing, transportation, and mining, instead of agriculture.

As the prerogatives of all elite lessen in the developmentally more advanced industrializing societies, the modernizing peasantries increasingly surrender part of their production to the impersonal bureaucracy of a partly industrialized state, rather than to members of the old elite. During the early stages of modernization of peasants, their social inferiority is more often a result of customary social relations than of the laws of a modernizing state (cf. Dalton 1972:406 and see also 393–394).

In the largely developed industrial state, government is invariably by elected or nominally elected representatives of all or most of its inhabitants, including the remaining postpeasants. However, the elected bureaucratic administrators are politically "attuned" to the wielders of industrial and commercial power, if they are not themselves the wielders of this power, as in the states with varying degrees of socialistic orientation. In the more democratized of these industrial states, political power is supposed to be held by the electorate, including the remaining folk and proletarians. Actually, relatively little power is exercised by the voter. Political power is instead exercised by elected political administrators, and by industrial-commercial administrators who have no mandate from or responsibility to the electorate. The loci of political power are more difficult to pinpoint in these more democratized industrial states, but, it is apparent that the near lack of power that the commoner experiences in the agrarian state often remains unchanged to a large extent in the industrial state. A major difference is that in these industrial states the new lower and middle classes have a higher standard of consumption than the old agrarian commoners. (On this last point, see Lundberg 1968.)

We will return to the modernization of peasants as the subject of the final chapter of this unit. Now we shall consider the peasant way of life more thoroughly. First the peasant as producer, then his systems of exchange will be discussed. After that we shall examine the political and social organization of peasant life.

3

Economics and Technology of Production in Peasant Society

The economics of production in peasant society and, as it relates to production, technology will be discussed in this chapter. By technology we mean the tools and techniques man uses to modify and control his environment. Here we review the way in which peasants use their productive resources, existing in limited quantity (such as land, labor, tools and other equipment, and techniques and other knowledge) to produce goods and services (such as grain, meat, pottery, houses, iron goods, and repairs to and alterations of goods). In the following chapter we shall also examine how peasants and others exchange these goods and services with other inhabitants of an agrarian state for purposes of consumption.

If asked what mental images first come to mind when the word peasant is used, one might well respond that he thinks of toiling cultivators in a field of green maturing plants, or perhaps of a sinewy plowman guiding his plow behind a straining pair of yoked oxen in a barren, brown field in early spring. When we think of peasants we usually think of self-sufficient tillers of the soil. It is to this tillage that we first turn our attention.

KINDS OF PRODUCTION FOUND AMONG PEASANTS

Most peasants make their livelihood primarily from the cultivation of domesticated plants for food, animal feed, and fibers and secondarily from the raising of livestock. Many have almost no livestock at all, and a scant few may be solely shepherds of animals found in peasant communities. Many peasants also engage part-time in production of crafts, rendering of services, or sometimes fishing, but some may engage in one of these activities as a full-time vocation. Peasants usually eke out a livelihood only a little above the subsistence level, using equipment energized by the power of humans and domesticated animals. The vast majority of those who are cultivators provide mainly for their family needs but also engage in some economic exchange of their production. Those who engage in noncultivating occupations to an appreciable extent must necessarily exchange their specialized production to satisfy family needs. Noncultivating peasants are given further consideration below, and we now discuss the technologies of peasants who are primarily cultivators.

Peasant cultivation is labor intensive rather than capital intensive, as is the case for the technologically advanced modern agriculturalists of industrial societies. Since peasant tools are technologically simple, techniques of production relatively inefficient, and arable land usually limited, labor is the only factor of production over which the peasant has even a modicum of control. To insure survival, a reliable supply of labor is needed. Hence, large families for ordinary tasks and social ties to others in the community for more laborious tasks are created. (These ties are examined in a following section on the social organization of peasants, and the global consequences of large peasant families are discussed in the final chapter.)

When he cultivates his land, the peasant is at the mercy of sun, wind, rain, hail, and frost, and this is equally true of modern agriculturalists. The peasant, however, has neither the scientifically developed, high-yield, and disease-resistant strains of plants and animals, nor the chemical fertilizers, herbicides, insecticides, and medicines for livestock available to the farmer, all of which help to insure successful yields. Thus the peasant runs a far greater risk of failure in realizing his productive yield than does the farmer or, for that matter, a cultivator on the tribal level who has greater recourse to hunting and gathering in uncultivated areas.

The technology of peasant cultivation may be classified as that of horticulture or of agriculture, both of which include the raising of livestock in conjunction with cultivation. Somewhat confusingly, these two specific terms are often lumped together under the generic term agriculture. This use of the word agriculture refers to *all* kinds of cultivation of plants and associated raising of livestock. In referring to the evolution and organization of agricultural civilization, we have used the word agriculture in this way. However, in the following discussion we use the term in its specific meaning.

HORTICULTURAL PRODUCTION

Horticulture, which is sometimes called gardening, is the technologically most primitive and the earliest form of cultivation. (Perhaps the only justifiable and nonethnocentric use of the term "primitive" as applied to an aspect of culture is with regard to technology, which has its own built-in standard of worth or ranking of intrinsic utility. In other words, either the technique or artifact "works better" or it does not, and it is thereby less or more primitive in a utilitarian frame of reference.) Horticultural technology consists of the use of hand tools powered by human muscles alone. Pointed digging sticks, hoes, or, more rarely, spades may be used to break and further cultivate the light soils of horticulture. Such tools cannot be used effectively on stiff, heavy soils rich in clay or in areas where a dense sod of matted grass roots covers the earth.

Actually, horticultural techniques are used exclusively by relatively few of the world's peasantries. Nevertheless, under favorable conditions horticulture may produce a yield equivalent to those of certain kinds of technologically more advanced agriculture. Agricultural peasants often have some garden plots of certain plants, which are tilled with horticultural techniques. Some peasants employing agricultural techniques may move to a different area and "revert" to using horticultural techniques if by so doing they can produce the same amount of crops with less energy. Also certain peasants must use horticulture in areas too rugged for the use of agricultural draft animals and the plow. In the arable land around many of the world's cities, peasants engage in horticultural production, usually in permanent and fertilized fields, of "table" vegetables and fruits for the consumption of urbanites.

However, most horticulture is not of this permanent kind, but is of the slash and burn, or swidden, variety. Here brush is cut and trees are ringed with a cutting tool in order to kill them, or they are sometimes more laboriously felled. The dried remains of this slashing are then set on fire, resulting in a cleared field of smoldering ashes and stumps. Minerals which fertilize the field are released from these ashes. As the fertility of a field wanes, the place of cultivation is relocated, after a few or many years. Either an area of virgin growth or a previously cleared area that has been abandoned and has "returned to nature" is slashed and burned. For this reason, this kind of horticulture is also referred to as shifting cultivation. Sometimes the community in which the cultivators live is fairly permanent and is located in the center of the "shifted" fields. More frequently, the community must be moved after a decade or two. Green manuring is a horticultural technique used less commonly than others to help fertilize the soil by turning under weeds and remains of domesticated plants so that they may decay in the ground. Fallowing of a field for a few years may also be used to restore the soil's fertility.

In horticulture two fundamentally different kinds of techniques of propagation exist—those of seeding and vegetative planting. Both of these techniques are also fundamental to the more advanced agricultural technology, and thus what we say here is relevant to all of peasant cultivation. In reproduction of plants through seeding, the seeds of a domesticate are either simply dropped or placed into the turned soil or are broadcast (strewn) by hand. In vegetative reproduction through planting, a piece of a domesticate is buried in a hole in the ground. This piece is a fragment of a vegetative organ of a plant. The organ may be a sprout, a cutting from a stem, a section of a divided root stock, or a segment of an underground tuber.

In planting, the domesticate grown is usually an identical reproduction of the single parent from which it is produced. This technique is one of asexual reproduction and, unlike seeding, does not involve the fusion of fertilization in pairs of sex cells (gametes). Associated with planting are the complex techniques of grafting, the forming of an organic union between two pieces of closely related plants. Many planted domesticates, for example the banana, have been vegetatively reproduced by man for so many millennia that their seeds are now sterile, having lost their viability or power to achieve fertilization.

Seeding is used for such crops as cereals, legumes, and the oil seeds of Southwest Asian origin, while planting is used for such crops as yams, taro, and other tuberous root crops and bananas of Southeast Asian origin. Certain crops use both basic techniques. Wet rice, cultivated by an incalculable number of Asian peasants, is first seeded into nursery beds and then transplanted by hand into a different field. Seeding and planting techniques have intermingled across much of the Old World, perhaps after diffusing from independent Southwest and Southeast Asian Neolithic centers of origin. Or, it could be that the two techniques are part of a dual and recurring pattern of human adaption to environment through the domestication of plants. Broadcast seeding and associated plow agriculture were introduced by Europeans to the Western Hemisphere, where they encountered an apparently indigenous horticultural complex of planting and simple drop seeding. (For additional information on planting and seeding see Sauer 1952.)

This horticultural complex is still found among the Mayan Indian peasants of Mexico:

The Mayas have been maize cultivators par excellence for some 4500 years, and the Zinacantecos are no exception. Not only does the overwhelming bulk of daily calories come from maize, but a proper meal without maize in some form is inconceivable to them (Vogt 1970:48).

The technology used in Zinacanteco farming is still fundamentally aboriginal in character. While they utilize a few steel tools—axes, machetes, bill hooks, and hoes—the farming techniques are those of swidden agriculture perfected centuries ago. The pattern is one of cutting down the trees and brush, burning them when dry, and then planting with a pointed digging stick. Fields are planted for varying periods of time, depending upon elevation and quality of the soil, and then allowed to grow into brush again. In the Highlands, where fertilization is practiced, the cycle is long; in the Lowlands, the cycle is much shorter where the parcels can be farmed for only three years, and then the fields must be moved, allowing the old parcels several years to lie fallow (Vogt 1970:50).

AGRICULTURAL PRODUCTION

The specific term agriculture may be usefully divided into two subspecific classifications. One of the two is concerned with the use of plow and draft animals and the other, which may or may not involve their use, centers upon irrigation of the fields. The first we call plow agriculture and the second hydraulic agriculture.

Plow Agriculture developed out of early Neolithic horticulture during the late Neolithic of Southwest Asia. Its introduction allowed two very important cultural adaptations to the geographic environment. The plow enabled men to turn denser soils and to cut the less heavy of the grassland sods, thus bringing more kinds of land into the Neolithic Revolution. Furthermore, this tool increases cultivating productivity, especially where the technique of broadcast seeding is employed. The plow is an energy converter which, when harnessed to draft animals, multiplies the effort of human muscle power.

Increase in the amount of land that one man can turn over in one day, the most arduous part of tillage, increases a group's productivity in crops. Increased agricultural productivity means a potential increase of agricultural surpluses, if sufficient incentive is present. Such an incentive in the form of edicts handed down by an emerging elite, wielding increasingly greater social power, helped usher in the Civilizing Revolution. Maintenance of this incentive, which we noted as the politically superior claim of the elite over the cultivator, resulted in a stabilization of the enthrallment of peasants. This social stabilization was within the political organization of the incipient state and then the state, down until the present time. And, of course, increased per capita production of crops creates increased means, through tax and sales, to support nonagricultural lifeways, especially those of the elite and their soldiers, scribes, and accountants, and also of craftsmen, merchants, and other occupations.

As population increased along with the development of plow agriculture, this technology opened virgin lands and provided the means to feed increases of population, to a certain limit. Eventually, the advent of the plow leads to population increase and pressures upon arable land, land scarcity, increase in the economic value of land, and increasing social differentiation of a population. This last takes place especially as control of land by a community or by a kinship group begins to be either replaced by or subordinated to ownership of land by a relatively few and

While his replacement grazes under the shade tree at right, an ox turns a horizontal wheel which through wooden cogs engages a vertical wheel carrying a belt of pots. These move downward into a sump connected to the canal in the foreground and then moving upward tip their water out into a channel leading to the irrigated fields in the background. This example of the animate energizing of machines in agrarian society is from the Fayum Depression in Egypt.

increasingly elitist families. Population pressures upon land and the need for maintenance of order in a growing and socially diversifying yet economically interdependent population necessitates greater political control by the leaders of the population. To this end an administrative elite, through its waxing political power, must apportion, regulate, maintain, and defend from outsiders land, labor, and, where present, irrigation systems. (Here we should note that the origin of incipient states in Southwestern Asia during the fourth millennium B.C. involved early plow agriculture and some amount of irrigation.) The emerging elite also coordinate and regulate exchange of crops and other goods between the economically interdependent groups in the proximity of the (early) irrigation sites.

Plow agriculture necessarily relies upon draft animals and therefore involves a much closer symbiotic relationship between men, plants, and animals than does any other form of cultivation. This relationship approximates a balanced, mixed husbandry of plants and animals, which is more adaptive to the environment than a single or nearly single husbandry involving plants only or animals only. In the mixed husbandry the draft animals plow, harrow, and cultivate the earth, thresh crops with their hooves, haul away the produce, and sometimes operate irrigation, grinding, or other simple machines. They consume the stalks and leafy remains of the crops in the fields, graze on fallowed fields, and are often allowed to return nutrients to the soil through deposition of their bodily wastes. However, many peasants must burn dung from their herbivores for fuel, as all fuels are in short supply in peasant society. Even when the domesticated animals do not return many nutrients to the soil, the plow itself retards depletion of the soil. As the plow cuts the earth it turns weeds under the soil, causing them to decompose into beneficial nutrients, and it also turns soil over, exposing to the surface nutrients which have percolated below the level of the roots of domesticated plants.

A vital tool in plow and hydraulic agriculture is the wheel. It is used not only to multiply the transportation capacity of domesticated pack and draft animals such as the ass and the ox, but also occasionally to harness wind and water power, and more commonly animal power for milling and the raising of water to cultivated fields. Heavier wheeled plows, cutting deeper into the earth and opening lands not entirely cultivable with the ordinary plow, were used in Europe north of the Mediterranean and then diffused to North America during its periods of colonization by Europeans.

Hydraulic Agriculture may use the hand tools of horticulture or the plow and draft animals of plow agriculture or combinations of both. However, it is differentiated from these two types by the extensive use of irrigation and the intensive application of human labor in cultivation. Southwest Asia undoubtedly first developed irrigated agriculture, but the most extensive hydraulic systems are found in southern and eastern Asia. The world's greatest population densities of peasants are those based upon hydraulic agriculture, as in Java, Japan, and central China.

Hydraulic agriculture may thus be found in arid and semiarid areas and in wet tropical areas. In either kind of ecological zone, an irrigation system must be constructed and kept in repair, including dikes, reservoirs, major channels of distribution, and feeder ditches to particular fields. In the dry areas of Asia and North Africa the water comes from lesser streams and springs and especially from large rivers, which also deposit rich alluvium held in suspension. In tropical Asia the heavy rains provide water in addition to that of the streams and rivers. Tropical hydraulic agriculture, with its transplanting by hand and frequent manual moving of water in muddy paddies, takes far more labor and yields a greater output per unit of land than does any other kind of peasant production.

Thomas Fraser's study of Malay peasants, who are both fishermen and hydraulic agriculturalists, succinctly depicts the productive technology of this kind of cultivation, its relation in the annual economic cycle to their production of fishing, and the reciprocal exchanges of labor in cultivation:

> Perhaps the most important reason that rice continues to be cultivated at all in these fishing villages is that the rains required to flood the rice fields occur with the northeast monsoon when the seas are too rough for any large-scale fishing.
>
> The first plowing of the *padi* fields is begun in July or August by men. . . . A heavy plow, *nanga*, pulled usually by one bullock, is required to break the dry and sun-caked soil. This operation may take a cultivator from two days to a week, as he works only during the early morning and late evening hours when the heat is less intense.
>
> Heavy plowing is followed by raking with the *gurah*, also pulled by a bullock, to break up the largest clods left from the plowing. Raking can usually be accomplished in one morning. The fields are now ready for seeding, which

simply involves broadcasting rice saved from the previous year's harvest over a selected seeding area or field (no more than a quarter of an individual's total holding). Until after the rains have started, and fishing stopped, this is all that is done.

By October, but continuing on into November, after sufficient rain has fallen to cover the rice fields and the seedlings have grown to a height of between 4 and 6 inches, one of the two periods of intense activity in the rice cycle begins, transplantation. Broadcasting the seed and transplanting are done by both sexes. For transplanting, it is desirable to assemble a group of a dozen or more people. Unlike most activities in Rusembilan, recruitment of groups to work in the rice fields is not on the basis of association among members of the same boat crew, but on the basis of kinship proximity. A man will first call on his own and his wife's closest relatives living in the village, then the next closest degree of relatives, and so on until he feels he has recruited sufficient labor for the task at hand. He recruits just enough labor, for not only must he feed those working on his fields, but he knows that by asking them to help him, he has assumed an obligation to reciprocate (Fraser 1966:14).

Modern Agriculture is a recent development which had its beginnings in Europe during the centuries just before the Industrial Revolution. The Second Agricultural Revolution, as the advent of modern agriculture is sometimes called, had antecedents in the various forms of traditional cultivation already discussed and in sociopolitical changes among European peasants. These changes included the breakdown of the feudal system in Western Europe, the compacting by peasants of a number of their traditional strip plots into a single, more rationally worked piece of family land, and, especially in England during the Industrial Revolution, the driving of peasants from their land (often so that it could be used to graze wool-producing sheep, as an adjunct to the expanding woolen textile mills).

Technological developments of the Second Agricultural Revolution include the introduction of new crops, many of which like maize and the "Irish" potato were brought to the Old World by European navigation. Of even greater significance was the development of scientific agriculture. Chemical and biological research and rational management of agriculture resulted in the introduction of chemical fertilizers, selective breeding of plants and animals, and more efficient use of traditional techniques of organic fertilization and cultivation. Developed also were the techniques of rotation of crops on a field (for example, from grain to clover, which fixes nitrogen in the soil) in order to replace the older land intensive technique of fallowing of fields to regain their fertility.

The mechanization of agriculture had its beginnings during this scientific development in the form of the iron plowshare and the horse-drawn "drilling" machine for deep seeding in even rows. However, the real mechanization of agriculture began after the mid-nineteenth century with the support of the advanced phases of the Industrial Revolution. Eventually, machines for plowing, harrowing, reaping, threshing, and transport were to become fuel-energized and ever more efficient in increasing productivity. Agricultural chemistry of fertilization and, in the twentieth century, protection of crops and stock against disease and pests further aided the development of modern agriculture.

Just as much as the Industrial Revolution, the Second Agricultural Revolution was essential for the beginnings of the replacement of masses of relatively self-sufficient, tradition-bound peasants with small numbers of modern agriculturalists producing specialized crops for other sectors of society. This replacement, began first in Western Europe and became markedly noticeable only in the nineteenth century. It is now in the process of aiding in the thus far relatively limited transformation of peasants either into modern agriculturalists, or, by forcing them out of cultivation, into modern types in nonagricultural occupations. Whether or not a majority of world peasants will be able to moderize their cultivation is a topic discussed in Chapter 7. We can say, however, that today, increasingly large numbers of the world's peasants are taking up at least some of the less capital intensive techniques of modern agriculture.

NONAGRICULTURAL PRODUCTION

As already mentioned, in addition to plant and animal production most peasants also produce craft goods and render services, gather wild plants for food and crafts, sometimes fish and, more rarely, hunt game. Some anthropologists have noted that certain rural producers who are not cultivators may be considered peasants (see Gamst 1970: 382). For example, in north-central Ethiopia, the analytic separation of rural craftsman from cultivator must be done arbitrarily and not based on ethnographic data. Here occupations of rural dwellers are discernable as a continuum of only slightly differentiated categories. These categories range from those who are agriculturalists producing crafts only for domestic consumption and during only a small part of the time, through numerous gradations, to those who are full-time producers of crafts and services for the market. Generally speaking, few of the world's peasants engage in agriculture to the exclusion of all other production, but some peasants engage in other rurally situated production to the exclusion of agriculture.

Rather than attempt to enumerate all of the nonagricultural divisions of productive labor relating to peasants and all of the kinds of crafts and services required by the world's peasants, we can gain some insight into this matter by examining the situation of the Qemant of Ethiopia and their Falasha and Muslim neighbors. Before their consumption by the Qemant, all foodstuffs produced by Qemant or others are processed within the Qemant family. In contrast, families of some of the world's peasantries have their grain ground or their oil seeds pressed by others who render these services as a means of earning a livelihood:

> No Qemant craftsmen produce goods for the market, but domestic crafts of several kinds are well developed. Women make baskets, using a coil technique, and, in the lowlands they also make mats of a checked pattern. Men make rope and twine of grass and animal hair, and they make querns and pestles of stone. Thatching of roofs and carpentry in constructing houses, furniture, and plows are also done by men. If a man is especially skilled in carpentry, he may do such work for a neighbor in return for goods or labor in his fields. Iron tools and pottery are obtained for goods or money from Falasha smiths, who are male, and potters, who are female. A Qemant woman spins her own cotton on a spindle whorl, twirling it in her hand. The thread thus spun is taken to a male Falasha or Muslim weaver, who produces cloth from it. Leather goods are acquired from a special occupational group of tanners . . . (Gamst 1969: 81).

The Falasha and many of the Muslims to varying extents are also plow agriculturists. The scope of the division of labor in nonagricultural production within agrarian society, including the degree of dependency of the peasant family and community on outsiders for crafts and services, varies from peasantry to peasantry. The extent of this kind of dependency is part of a larger question fundamental to the understanding of the nature of peasant ways of life. To what extent are peasants economically self-sufficient? In order to better understand the matter of the degree of independence or dependence of peasants, we shall now examine their systems of exchange.

4
Economics of Exchange in Peasant Society

Social systems of economic exchange are only one aspect of a peasant society, but they are vital for comprehension of peasant life. Exchange systems are joined with those of production and consumption to comprise the economic subsystem of a society, and these are interrelated with components of other societal subsystems. Thus we may analytically consider any or all of these three economic aspects apart from other social subsystems, but in ethnographic reality economics is intertwined with sociocultural limitations and conditions. These are imposed by other subsystems including bonds of kinship, requirements of religion, and controls of politics.

Systems of exchange in a peasant society are of several kinds and may be thought of as social networks linking individuals and groups to one another within a community and, very often, to a wider extracommunity network. This wider social network may simply unite several neighboring communities or may comprehend an entire region, or perhaps all of the regions of a state. It sometimes encompasses other states as well, and, sometimes, in the case of market exchange, includes some degree of union with the price-making global network of market exchange, which has only recently developed.

Traditional peasant society is partially defined in terms of one of the three principle kinds of exchange: marketing, redistribution, and reciprocity. This definition is inclusive of a peasantry in a partially developed, hence small-scale, regional or larger system of market exchange. Goods and services resulting from peasant production and later to be consumed or used by peasants are exchanged to varying but usually limited extents in such markets. This is in contrast to most industrial societies dominated by and totally organized around markets which are consequently of a large scale. (The internal economies of Communist industrial states such as the Soviet Union may be considered more redistributive than market. Here the state collects from productive associations of all kinds and then redistributes goods and services thus realized to the various socioeconomic sectors of its society.) An additional contrast between traditional peasant societies and most industrial societies is that land and labor, the two basic elements of agricultural production, are only rarely exchanged in peasant marketing systems.

Traditional peasant marketing, then, is on a small scale, that is, the market does not provide the primary dynamic of social interaction, as it does in most industrial societies. In other words, classic peasant economics are not organized largely around markets, and classic peasants engage in a considerable amount of their exchange outside the market. However, as they develop into the postpeasants of most industrializing states, they gradually become more attuned to the pulse of the market. Others develop into postpeasants of a collective type, existing apart from marketing to some extent as in the Soviet Union.

Such a characterization of peasant-agrarian economy differentiates it from an industrial one, but does not differentiate it from many of the tribal economies (cf. Dalton 1972:388–392). It is only with the addition of the superordinate elite and subordinate commoner distinction of asymmetrical relations of power in economic exchange, within the organization of a civilized state, that we are able to analytically differentiate the peasant from the tribalist. The focus of these relations of power are found in various systems of agrarian land tenure. In these systems "rent" is rendered by the peasant not just as a material payment but as an expression of the ideological and social maintenance of the dual-asymmetrical organization of the state (cf. Wolf 1972:411).

Following the work of the economic historian Karl Polanyi (1957), and others (see Dalton 1971) who build upon his ideas, we realize that at least two other modes of exchange, redistribution and reciprocity, are interrelated with market exchange in peasant society. We shall now examine each of these three modes of exchange found among peasants.

MARKET EXCHANGE

By market exchange is meant the exchange of goods and services at prices regulated by supply and demand. Truly "free" markets with prices regulated only in this manner and not by some degree of other controls are rare, if they have ever existed at all. Markets generally became predominant over the other two modes of exchange when a developed and enforceable law of contract exists, as in the industrial states, with their comprehensive written legal codes and nearly universal literacy.

Before European commercial and military expansion over the globe by means of its preindustrial technology of navigation, a number of restricted, interstate areas of trade existed. These areas, varying in size, were segments of continents and were linked into a price-making global market network as a consequence of the European expansion during the past several centuries. Today, the economic effect of this nearly completed world marketing system is increasingly far reaching as forces of the modernized market structurally change and condition lifeways of more and more peasants.

Some present-day peasants have an "insulating" adaptation to the global market. When prices fall for crops produced for exchange upon the world market, some peasants can and do reduce production of these commodities and increase production of subsistence crops. Thus, the peasant protects himself from fluctuations in and manipulation of the world market by withdrawing to his community and regional markets, or to nonmarket exchange. This insulation is more difficult or becomes impossible to achieve as the peasant community becomes dependent upon certain goods and services obtainable only through the world market. Insulation also fades away when land is irrevocably committed to long-term cash crops such as bananas, hemp, coffee, and other tree crops.

In peasant marketing, goods necessary to the maintenance of peasant life are

A female Falasha Agaw potter finishing a traditional coffee pot of Bagemder Province, Ethiopia, by burnishing it with water and a pebble before firing it. Peasant producers of crafts in much of the world have lost or are losing their economic niches as artisans because of the introduction of cheap manufactured goods from outside industry.

exchanged, sometimes through middle-men who are frequently little removed from the peasants; but often they are purchased by the consumer from the actual producer of the foodstuff, fiber, or craft good. Sometimes this marketing is not monetized, that is, goods or services are exchanged, but money is not a medium of this exchange for the literally penniless peasants. Because of the poverty, and hence the limited purchasing power of peasants and other folk, exchange is in small amounts: a basket of cotton, a paper cone of coffee or of salt, a pinch or two of several spices, one pot, or one piece of iron ware. Not only is the size of the transaction small, but goods are of a rather limited variety. (In rural Ethiopia, one can purchase a pot of any color one desires—just so long as that color is brown.) Goods cannot be too heavy or bulky because of the transport limitations of humans and pack animals. Furthermore, goods cannot be too intricate or require a large amount of capital or labor in production because of the respective limitations of the peasant's technical knowledge and of his purse. For example, peasants cannot maintain or purchase tractors without outside assistance.

During the past century, increasing amounts of easily portable and fairly inexpensive goods from industrial states have been pumped into local and regional peasant markets. In return, the collective wealth of the peasants' pennies is pumped back into the industrial centers. With this increase of industrial goods began the still continuing decrease in the production of local and regional preindustrial craft wares. These were once the only kind available in small-scale peasant marketing. In this way, modern industry is destroying the viability of peasant cottage industry for both the part-time and the full-time craftsman. Generally, more efficient goods are industrially produced *and* distributed to be sold cheaper than those made by hand. Thus one economic prop of many peasantries, the supplementing of subsistence agriculture with returns from handicrafts, is undermined at the same time that scientific public health allows greatly increased population pressure upon the land.

One adjunct to small-scale peasant markets is often the "renting" of money at very high rates of interest to peasants who need a loan in order to continue their annual round of activities. Thus usury, the lending of money and, at times, the advance of goods at exhorbitant rates of interest, may be viewed as a totally nonredistributive "tax" upon many peasants, and especially upon those experiencing the pressures of the monetized global market. Individual members of the elite and also burgher merchants and money lenders may advance money or goods such as seed grain or capital equipment to a peasant family. Repayment at usurious rates is made at harvest time.

To understand better a traditional peasant system of marketing, we turn to the Qemant for illustration of a large number of marketing patterns found throughout agrarian civilization. In our passages on the Qemant, we shall note that market exchange may be usefully considered as consisting of two kinds of transactions, formal and informal. We shall also see that market exchange is not solely related to the marketplace and may be transacted outside of it. A marketplace is distinct from marketing (a form of exchange) and is a location in space and time where formal marketing transactions are conducted. An example of such a locus is the Wednesday market, a part of a regional ring of marketplaces, in Qemantland. (Often each part of the common ring marketplace specializes in one or more goods, for example, salt, cotton, pottery, or certain foodstuffs, in addition to the exchange of more general items.) We should further note in the passages on the Qemant, the use and nonuse of money and the range of its form in marketing, functions of a marketplace besides those of exchange, the existence of ring (or sectional or cyclical) marketplaces, the kinds of material dependency of the Qemant peasant upon the market, and the kinds of traders in the marketplace:

> A large part of Qemant exchange is not transacted within their interesting, busy marketplaces and, as we shall see, their marketplaces bustle with activities other than trade.
> *Formal Marketing* Means of transportation and communication in the Qemant region are poorly developed, and the Qemant peasant has access only to his own regional market system, which is little affected by conditions outside Qemant society. . . .
> Money is almost always used in formal marketing and is sometimes employed in informal marketing. Today the official Ethiopian copper and paper currency is used as the principal medium of exchange. Although they are not official currency of the nation, silver Maria Theresa coins, minted in Austria during the late 1700s and thereafter, are still used, and some people hoard them because of their silver content. Salt bars, an ancient medium of exchange that was replaced by modern coinage about fifty years ago, might still be regarded as a minor medium of exchange since they are conventionally used to reward priests for certain of their services.
> Formal marketing is held at fixed times in marketplaces, usually little more than vacant clearings when the market is not being held. Until a decade ago,

markets were held once a week in uncultivated areas of Qemant communities and sometimes in or near administrative villages of the Amhara, and were part of a regional weekly cycle of markets that covered six days of the week. Two former marketplaces in Karkar are still called Monday market . . . and Friday market. . . . A Wednesday market . . . is still operated. . . . The Saturday market is still held in nearby Gondar Town. Today, administrative and market villages . . . have replaced older marketplaces in many parts of the Qemant area. . . . The most important marketplace for [the province of] Bagemder and Semen has existed since about 1600 and is in the town of Gondar which now has a daily market in addition to the older, major market on Saturday.

For the Qemant peasant, trading at a marketplace is a means of exchanging a commodity of which he has a slight surplus for another commodity which he lacks. Occasionally, services are performed, as when tanners in the marketplace cover storage baskets with leather. Commodities that the Qemant need include some otherwise unobtainable plant products, such as cotton from the lowlands; mineral products available only in distant areas, such as salt from the Danakil Depression; and products, such as Falasha iron ware, of local crafts in which the Qemant do not engage. Machinemade goods, originating abroad or in Ethiopian cities, are rare in markets except those in towns and villages on the main provincial road. Traders in town markets . . . and in village markets include Ethiopian and Arab full-time middlemen and some peasants selling a part of their surplus. In marketplaces in the countryside, the few full-time traders are usually itinerants, and local peasants do most of the selling.

To Market, To Market, To Hear the Late News   The marketplace functions for the Qemant in other ways besides exchange. Most important, it provides a sort of social glue for the Qemant. Married women, who live among their husbands' kin, are reunited and may gossip with their siblings and former neighbors during not-so-chance meetings in the marketplace. Relatives and friends have a legitimate excuse, buying or selling, to take a day off from labor in the home or fields and to catch up on the latest happenings to one another. A vendor may not sell all of her produce, but no matter, for going to market is always exhilarating, even without sales or purchases. In general, the centers of trade are homogenizers of ideas and modes of behavior, for one perceives here how members of local and distant communities are acting and thinking. In short, the marketplace greatly increases, on a regular basis, the number of face-to-face contacts a peasant can maintain.

In the marketplace, one might additionally see or learn of strangers in the community and hear the latest of the customary pronouncements from the local feudal officials. These officials have long guaranteed the peaceful existence of the marketplace so that their region will prosper, and produce taxes, through trade and commercial traffic to centers of trade. Through control and surveillance of markets, local officials can feel the pulse of their territory and stay attuned to the moods of the populace.

Informal Marketing   Informal marketing consists of exchange between two persons in which middlemen are not involved, and money is seldom used. This trade may be transacted anywhere in a community at almost any time. In most transactions, a certain amount of one commodity is deemed equal in value to a certain amount of another commodity and the two are exchanged. Before livestock is exchanged, however, the price is agreed upon in Maria Theresa dollars. If one of the parties in the transaction receives an animal worth less than the one he has given, he receives additional produce priced at the number of Maria Theresas needed to balance the exchange (Gamst 1969:81–83).

Informal marketing involves a loosely defined and structured social network of irregularly and often temporarily interacting trading partners. Goods and services so exchanged may be restricted to the community or the region, but some may eventually enter markets on the interstate or even global level. In many peasant communities and regions, informal marketing may once have accounted for a greater amount of exchange than formal marketing. This informal marketing includes nonpeasant commoners of the regions involved.

STATUS ECONOMICS

Reciprocal and redistributive exchange are often closely intertwined with status and are therefore often called status economics, as opposed to market economics. When considering these two kinds of status economies, activities of exchange are understandable only in light of the social positions and related roles of people in their society. For example, kinsmen, comembers of associations, members of castes, and neighbors within communities reciprocate goods and services with others in relation to the rights and duties of their statuses in their societies, and not just with regard to economizing considerations.

Of course, maximization of income is certainly one basic strategy of the life style of each peasant family, but this strategy is rarely given free reign or expressed independently. Thus reciprocities, such as those involving labor and ceremonial occasion, and outlooks, such as apprehension over a neighbors' negative reaction to one's "getting ahead," temper a peasant's realization of self-interest. Such socially tempered behavior is frequently cited as a lack of rationality or reasoning on the part of peasants, especially by "urbane, enlightened agents of modernization" who are frustrated in their attempts to initiate a developmental program involving these "benighted rustics." The problem is not a lack of comprehension by peasants of what is "good for them," but rather, enculturation within a different cognitive frame, which engenders close personal relations and the balancing of social costs at the expense of economizing tendencies (see Foster 1962).

RECIPROCAL EXCHANGE

Reciprocity is the exchange of goods and services between social units that are similar in organization, but not necessarily equally ranked. It takes place outside the market and outside the social organizations of redistribution. Reciprocal exchange is transacted between pairs of social units ranging from individuals through intermediate levels of social organization (such as families, larger kinship groups, castes, and communities) to, in some instances, the level of entire societies. Examples of this kind of exchange include reciprocity between two peasant families having the same amount of wealth, or between a prosperous townsman and a poor peasant, or between a high-ranked caste group and one low-ranked. Although some of the most common systems of peasant reciprocity are informally organized between either a number of persons or a number of families, reciprocity is frequently found among those peasants who create a formal group that is a common interest association focusing upon mutual aid. The association usually exchanges labor and sometimes capital equipment such as plows and draft animals for agricultural purposes. At times, these associations include nonagricultural activities, for example, the building of houses. All of these exchanges may be on a regular basis and thus foster a normal, partially cooperative means of production in a community, or they may operate only as a form of "insurance" of productive yields and thus be activated only in time of individual or family need or hardship.

Networks of reciprocity are usually extendable according to the requirements of the situation. However, the potential for greatly developed systems of reciprocity does not necessarily result in the total self-sufficiency of a peasant community. At this point we should note that among peasants considerable amounts of foodstuffs, as well as other goods and services, are reciprocated within and between communities at the time of various rites of passage[1] of individuals and other ceremonial occasions. Families and common interest associations focusing upon ceremony are the social units of this wide-spread reciprocity. We will look at the Qemant again to view their networks of reciprocity and some of the kinds of things reciprocated. This selection concerns a common-interest association of men, which they call simply enough "my association":

> A group of men of approximately the same age form an association whose membership may change through time. Membership provides pleasurable fellowship, centering upon shared food and drink, labor for construction and agriculture, aid when one is involved in a dispute, and individual guarantors when needed in litigation. The members also form a pool to lend oxen, tools, seed grain, and money to one another. They contribute food and labor for members' rites of passage, particularly the rite for admission to heaven. Reciprocity is the keynote of membership. If a member does not "balance his account" with other members of the association over a period of time, he is warned first and then eventually expelled from the group (Gamst 1969:76–77).

Reciprocity between ritual, or fictive, kinsmen is an important kind of exchange in peasant society, where "actual" kinship is usually less important and all-enveloping than in tribal societies. We treat kinship of all kinds at greater length in Chapter 6, but here we should touch upon the economic aspects of systems of ritual kinship. Thus we turn to the *compadrazgo* system found throughout Latin America (see Buechler and Buechler 1971:46–49; Lewis 1960:66–68; Vogt 1970: 63–65), and with parallels in Mediterranean Europe, the area of origin of this form of ritual kinship. *Compadrazgo* not only extends a peasant's network of kinship for purposes of local sociopolitical alliance, but it is often specifically focused upon reciprocal exchange, and always has this as one of its functions. It may join two families of approximately the same rank, or it may be used to "cement" a patron-client relationship between a poor peasant and a more wealthy peasant, or perhaps a townsman. Oscar Lewis' classic ethnology of *Tepoztlan: Village in Mexico* gives us a good overview of *compadrazgo*:

> The system of *compadrazgo* establishes two sets of formal relationships between nonrelatives: the one is between "spiritual" godparents (*padrinos*) and their godchildren (*ahijados*); the other a relationship known as *compadres* or co-parents, is between the parents and the godparents. The general purpose of godparents is to provide security for the godchild. The godparents are in effect an additional set of parents who will act as guardians and sponsors of the godchild, care for him in emergencies, and adopt him if he is orphaned. In

---

[1] A rite of passage is a ceremony marking the change from one status to another in a person's life. Among the more common are rites of birth, puberty, marriage, and death. (See Buechler and Buechler 1971:79–83; Gamst 1969:99–115; and Vogt 1970:62–77 for ethnographic details of several kinds of these rites.)

Tepoztlan, however, the relationship between *compadres* is much more functional and important than that between the godparent and godchild.

They [*compadres*] do often exchange favors, and borrowing between them is probably more frequent than between kin. At the death of one *compadre* the other is supposed to contribute toward the funeral expenses. *Compadres* invite each other to barrio fiestas and treat each other with special deference. Tepoztecans prefer *compadres* who are neither neighbors nor relatives; most *compadres* come from other barrios.

Social, economic, and political factors may enter into the operation of the *compadre* system. Poor families look for better-to-do godparents for their children. Similarly it is thought desirable to have a *compadre* from the city for it is assumed that a city family can be of greater help in time of need. The more godchildren a man has, the more *compadres* and the wider circle of persons who can be counted on for favors (Lewis 1960:66–68).

An important example of reciprocity within the community is found in the traditional, and now transformed, prerevolutionary Russian *mir* (meaning both "world" and "peace"), or village commune, of which there were often more than one to a village. Many *mirs* reciprocated internally almost to the point of complete self-sufficiency and virtually all were considerably self-sufficient:

Historically, from about 1000 A.D., the basic form of land tenure and social organization among peasants in the central provinces was the *mir* or peasant commune. The *mir* consisted of a group of households, each of which had the right by virtue of its membership to hold plots of land in various categories (crop land, pasture, hay field, forest lot, and so on). Tenure was vested in the *mir* as a whole, however, and the land was subject to periodic redistribution among the constituent households, usually adult males. The assembly was known as the *skhod*, from the verb *skhodit'*, meaning to come together. Through its agent, the *starosta* (literally "elder"), the *skhod* conducted all transactions with individuals (or other social units) and with the state on behalf of its members. The *skhod* was responsible also for the collection of certain taxes from *mir* members and for their fulfillment of military and other obligations (Dunn and Dunn 1967:9).

Undoubtedly one of the most interesting forms of reciprocity within the community and one which very often comes close to maximum self-sufficiency is that of the *jajmani* system of reciprocal exchange (cf. Lewis and Barnouw 1956). It is the economic aspect of the caste system of social organization for hundreds of millions of peasants in India. In this socioeconomic system, families of the various caste groups of a community render services and furnish or loan goods according to obligations and rights peculiar to the caste. Until recently, very little money was used in *jajmani* exchange. The bonds of exchange are hereditary between each of two reciprocating caste groups, and on a family-to-family basis.

Nominal *jajmani* obligations are not always strictly defined or followed. Despite this fact, the system stabilizes the supply and division of labor in a community. Further, it provides a pool of poorly compensated, trained workers to the members of the power-wielding agricultural castes. They control the cultivable land, and usually local government and local aspects of certain religions. Of course, each nonagricultural caste group also reciprocates services with caste groups other than the higher and more powerful castes. Although the *jajmani* system is on the decline today, it is nevertheless still entrenched in India. The working of the *jajmani* system is readily seen in Alan Beals' account of *Gopalpur: A South Indian Village*:

Because Gopalpur contains only a fraction of the total spectrum of jatis [castes] and is dominated by jatis of approximately equal status, the economic significance of jati membership lies not so much in the restrictions that jati membership places upon an individual's capacity to improve his economic position, as in guaranteeing economic cooperation outside the family circle. For the farmer, it is good business to be on good terms with someone who owns a large flock of sheep, for this provides access to a source of manure. Basketweavers, Carpenters, and Blacksmiths are sources of farm equipment. Delay in repairing a cart or plow, or inability to obtain a basket to carry manure to the fields, can make the difference between the success or failure of agricultural operations. Typically, the farmer is rich at harvest time, poor at sowing time. He must depend upon goodwill and credit in order to survive.

For essential services, the farmer tends to enter into a contractual relationship with the specialist. The Carpenter, Blacksmith, Barber, and Potter receive fixed quantities of grain at harvest time. In return, they provide services. Most individuals in Gopalpur wash their own clothing; a few have a permanent arrangement with the Washerman. The priests of the various deities do not ordinarily receive a fixed amount. They tend to be given grain in accordance with the quality of the harvest. . . .

The magnificent generosity of the harvest season enables the farmer to purchase the goodwill, credit, and protection that will enable him to carry on long after his grain storage bins are empty and long after the generosity of the harvest season has been replaced by the bleak stinginess of the man who lives on credit. Most people in Gopalpur are farmers who occasionally supplement their income by taking advantage of traditional specializations and privileges. The fact that the Farmer jati maintains friendly relationships with the Carpenter jati is easily explained in economic terms. The fact that the Farmer jati maintains friendship with the Saltmaker jati is not so easily explained. Saltmakers produce very little salt. In any case, salt can be purchased at any little shop in any village or town. Saltmakers and Farmers are both farmers and there is no real necessity for an exchange of services. People say, we must be friendly with all other jatis because each of the other jatis contributes something essential to our economic well-being. This is what people say to each other, but it is not altogether true.

To fill the gap between reality and the ideal pattern of economically cooperating jatis, there are social and religious obligations. To arrange a marriage, to set up the doorway of a new house, to stage a drama, or to hold an entertainment, the householder must call upon a wide range of jatis. The entertainment of even a modest number of guests requires the presence of the Singer. The Potter must provide new pots in which to cook the food; the Boin from the Farmer jati must carry the pot; the Shepherd must sacrifice the goat; the Crier, a Saltmaker, must invite the guests. To survive, one requires the cooperation of only a few jatis; to enjoy life and do things in the proper manner requires the cooperation of many (Beals 1962:39–41).

REDISTRIBUTIVE EXCHANGE

The concept of redistribution has two elements. One is inflow, that is, the movement of certain goods and services to a center of an administrative organization, or else, not the actual movement but the control of goods and services by such an organization. The second element is outflow, that is, the reallotment of some part of these goods and services to the individuals encompassed by the redistributive organization.

Taxation resulting from the superior claim of the elite over the peasantry and other commoners of the agrarian state is one very significant form of redistribution, as is any taxation, including that of citizens of an industrial state by its impersonal governmental bureaucracy. Among the Qemant, as with other peasantries, we find that taxes are paid in kind, money, and labor to the state and provide the inflow of the state's redistributive system. The two most important items of the return or outflow of the state's redistribuion are maintenance of internal order and tranquility for the peasants and protection of them from external social power.

Redistributive exchange also exists apart from the central taxing authority of the state. Thus peasants might be within a community or a multicommunity network of redistribution administered by regional or local secular or religious authorities. As we have seen in the Russian *mir*, a "council of elders" of a peasant community, or else of some part of a community such as a clan or other group, may periodically or continuously redistribute land. Again, as with other peasantries, additional systems of redistribution are found in the religious organization of the Qemant. Religion for the Qemant is formally organized around their indigenous pagan-Hebraic faith and their more recent Ethiopian Orthodox Church. Both of these religious organizations collect in kind, money, and labor and redistribute some part of this wealth for the benefit of their congregations. The benefits include conducting periodic public ceremonies for the entire community, aiding the poor, organizing religious feasts for the rites of passage of individuals, and, more indirectly, maintaining priests for general service to the public—counseling of individuals, instruction in religious and other matters, and mediation of disputes.

AN OVERVIEW OF EXCHANGE AMONG PEASANTS

Having completed our discussion of peasant production and distribution, we may now attempt to resolve what may be considered a basic problem in understanding peasants and their place in our modernizing world. The literature in many studies on peasantries flatly states, or else implies through certain information, that their communities are economically self-sufficient. Other studies state that their communities are economically interdependent with a wider world.

Our selection of one of these statements or viewpoints over the other is first of all partly dependent upon the emphasis and interests of the social scientist, or journalist or novelist for that matter, who wrote about the particular peasants with whom we are concerned. A certain emphasis and related selection by the writer of particular data may give a distorted account of peasant self-sufficiency. Selection of one of these viewpoints necessarily varies in part with the community's degree of modernization, for this process brings about increased involvement in the monetized global market and thus a genuine loss of self-sufficiency. When peasants are ensnared in the global market, during the course of modernization, they often then supplement their income by part-time wage labor for wealthier peasants, urban households, commercial farms, or other commercial firms. This leads to further loss of self-sufficiency for the peasant.

Besides the outlook of the writer and the degree of modernization of the community, selection of one of the viewpoints must ultimately depend upon an analysis of the actual social and economic conditions of a particular peasant culture. Such analysis should take into account the amount of exchange conducted in each of the three systems of allocation discussed in this section. Comparative analysis of this kind for all peasantries will show many cases of highly developed reciprocal systems on the level of the community. In some of these cases a community can become free of the market, and where state control is weak, it can also often become free of redistribution above the level of community. Only with regard to such peasant communities (invariably of the classic type) can an empirical basis be found for statements on the independence and self-sufficiency of the peasant community.

In order to exist, most of the world's peasantries must exchange agricultural or other goods for differing amounts of necessary craft goods and services in the market towns of their region. Despite the existence of well-developed systems of reciprocity allowing near self-sufficience in many peasant communities, including the Russian *mir* and the *jajmani* system within Indian villages, exchange is supplemented by the market in virtually every instance, even if only to a very small extent. Thus a community may exhibit considerable internal reciprocity, yet be dependent upon the outside world for maintenance of its well being, for example, in the supplying of a few all-important goods, such as iron tools.

5

The Peasant Community and Its Relations with the Larger Society

We turn our attention in this chapter and the following one to social relations and their underlying social organizations, both within the peasant sector and between it and the rest of an agrarian state. In this chapter we shall focus especially upon the political aspect and in the following chapter upon kinship, associational, and other aspects of social organization. We shall examine the peasant community and its local, or internal, social organizations and relationships. We will also investigate the horizontal, or intercommunity, extensions of these local organizations to similar organizations of other peasant communities. Necessary for our understanding of peasantries as a sector of agrarian society is a tracing of the vertical organizations between subordinated peasants and superordinated elite and, at times, burghers.

We begin with an examination of the peasant community, followed by a discussion of social control in the peasant community and of the vertical dimension of peasant politics, including peasant insurrections. The related chapter which follows will deal with the peasant family and other social groupings of peasants.

THE PEASANT COMMUNITY

Following the classification of George P. Murdock (1949:80), most local communities of peasants are nucleated villages, with homesteads clustered together in the midst of economically exploited fields. Some are instead neighborhoods, with units of one or several homesteads dispersed at varying distances across the cultivated countryside. Many of the Qemant and Amhara communities of peasants in Ethiopia, for example, are neighborhoods.

In introducing our section on peasant production, we evoked the mental image of a self-reliant, toiling cultivator of the soil. A political addition to the average person's image of a peasant would undoubtedly be that of a cultivator "fettered" to the land and who owes part of his production to a superior of some kind. This image is largely correct, for a peasant is controlled in his local community by the elite of a state, which may be thought of as the greater community in which the peasant also lives.

Just as peasant villages and neighborhoods range economically from near self-sufficiency to a relatively great dependency upon the market, politically they range from near autonomy to strict subordination to the administrative hierarchy of the state. As Lloyd Fallers (1961:109) has succinctly explained, in the peasant community some amount of each of two political dimensions is always present. One dimension is that of local relations, where formal and informal local mechanisms of social control are used. These are established patterns of individual and collective behavior for regulating conduct, which are oriented to and regulated by the community with its Little Tradition. The other dimension is of vertical relations, where ascending levels of administrative organizations link the community to the apex of government and its written legal code rooted in centuries of Great Tradition juridical development. Either dimension may wax or wane through time in relation to the other. In modernizing agrarian states the vertical dimension becomes predominant.

At times, then, some communities of peasants may be almost politically and economically independent of any larger social order. These communities may therefore approximate what Wolf (1957) has depicted as a "closed corporate peasant community." Here we find "parochial, localocentric attitudes" and a greater display of apprehension by community members over any involvement with the outside world than is shown by members of more "open" communities. And thus we also find a discouragement of "close participation of members in the social relations of the larger society" (Wolf 1957:2). Undoubtedly all classic peasant communities displayed at least a moderate amount of closure or localocentrism, and this is also found to lesser degrees in modernizing peasant communities.

THE LOCAL POLITICS OF SOCIAL CONTROL

Despite the existence of "closed" communities we may say that peasant communities are never *entirely* closed or isolated and are always tied into a larger social order—that of the state. However, viewing things comparatively, these communities differ greatly in the extent to which they are bound by the state's political institutions. Life styles of a particular peasantry may be markedly different from that of another peasantry in significant part because of the contrastive severity or looseness of the political bindings of the state. Examples of this are the serfs of Czarist Russia who were tightly bound to the land as contrasted with those Qemant peasants who till a modestly taxed plot of what approximates communal freehold land, and whose local mechanisms of social control are well developed. Such mechanisms to some extent maintain behavioral norms and a social equilibrium in the community. Local mechanisms of this kind vary from those effected by an entire community, to special groups, to particular statuses in the community.

Even within a strong state, politics may occur apart from government and political institutions within the community which are linked in some way to government. Local political processes are a function of institutions which may or may not be primarily political in nature. Among other things, they may be primarily religious, recreational, or economic. For example, at times a reciprocal work association of peasants may affect governmental and nongovernmental political processes in the community, especially when its interests are at stake. Additionally, it should be noted, the association has its own internal "politicking," when its leaders are chosen, when its goals are agreed upon, or when its resources are allocated. Such "politics" internal to a group within a community are often microcosms of localized politics and, when the group is powerful enough, may overlap community politics.

Part of the local dimension of politics are judicial bodies organized to maintain harmony in the community. For example, among the Qemant we not only find politico-religious leaders as political adjuncts of the state, but outside of government, we find local mechanisms in the form of councils of elders with judicial powers (Gamst 1969:57–64). These councils are either permanently standing bodies or specially created for a particular purpose and then disbanded.

Through political organizations similar to these, or simply through extraorganizational, informal mechanisms—such as mediation by a third party or pressure of community opinion for maintenance of social tranquility—peasants frequently stay outside of the legal system and courts of the state. Other informal, extraorganizational mechanisms include magic, witchcraft, invocation of the wrath of the gods, ostracism, open hostility projected by one's fellow community members, and public recitation of customary standards of conduct. In these ways peasants also stay outside of the grasp of state administrators, whose adjudications frequently include infliction of cruel and unusual punishment, and who invariably are not appreciative of the lifeways of peasants and of the personal dignity of individuals who are folk. However, sometimes peasants resort to the judicial system of the state for seemingly insoluable disputes and for very grave crimes such as murder (for example, see Gamst 1969:63–64).

Informal and formal mechanisms of social control on the local level usually tend to preserve the peace rather than to punish an "evildoer." Strong punishment, as any peasant knows, may unleash an unending chain of vendettas between families, between kinship organizations such as clans, and even between communities. Thus, frequently and freely used, strong sanctions may actually increase rather than retard social unrest and tension in a community. Recourse to coercion is usually reserved for the most uncontrollable or the potentially most disruptive of agressors who endanger the normally changing social order. Among the Qemant we note the struggle to preserve peace by a typical local judicial body of peasants, in this case a permanent council of elders:

On an appointed meeting day, the bearded, gray-haired elders, clad in togas, walk across the fields and assemble in a cleared area between the roots of two large trees. While the council members repose with vessels of beer under the canopy of trees, the council leader arranges for a guarantor, selected from assembled kith and kin, for each of the litigants. Any fines to be levied pass through the guarantor, who is responsible for payment. Erada and the other council members then hear evidence in separate hearings from each party to the dispute. This action prevents disruption of the judicial procedure arising from arguments between litigants and their witnesses.

From the hearings, the council members learn that last year the young man paid the older man Eth. $16.00, an advance two-thirds payment for the horse. The older man had decided to keep the horse until the final payment was made. When the young man had saved the remaining eight dollars of the purchase price of Eth. $24.00, he offered the money to the old peasant who then professed no knowledge of the original transaction. Following many weeks of meetings covering several hours each week, Erada and the other elders present their decision to the litigants: "The old man must return the money or complete the transaction." As often happens, the older peasant refuses to accept the council's judgment. When either litigant refuses to accept a decision (an unaccepted judgment is not binding), the elders hold additional hearings, leading to further deliberations.

The old man becomes recalcitrant, refusing to attend further hearings, now being held without him. For many months, the council requests the old man to appear, but he is adamant. Finally, the council decides to invoke their customary sanction. The old man receives a message stating, "Appear before council or we will curse you." This malediction is effected by pouring a sacred beer (meski) onto the earth in the name of the accursed one. Rather than receive the ultimate punishment, the old man finally agrees to come to court and, finally, to complete the transaction—for two dollars more than the original purchase price.

As is customary when a litigant finally accepts a judgment, partially or wholly against him, the old man places a stone on the back of his neck, bows to the younger man, and says, "Pardon me." The other litigant thereupon reciprocates with precisely the same ritual. The two then kiss one another on both cheeks and are blessed by Erada and the other elders of the council (Gamst 1969:60).

Despite local and vertical social controls and safeguards, strife does, of course, break out in peasant communities. Sometimes violence is not entirely dysfunctional for the community and may somewhat readjust community equilibrium, while reducing social and individual psychic tensions. Some of my ethnographic field notes concerning the Amhara of Ethiopia provide such an example. I came across this example while combing the notes for data to present the reader with an idyllic scene of social equilibrium and local law and order in a peasant community. Rather than idyllize peasant life in the often presented, romantic vein, we now put on our untinted glasses and recount the following case of what might well be called an example of "violent interpersonal relations as informal community control":

Among the Amhara, Qemant, and other neighboring peasantries (as among many of the world's peasantries), one person may try belligerently to increase his share of honor and prestige in the community at the expense of others. Such a person was Neguse the dulaña (one who fights with a staff, as in the familiar Anglo folk epic of Robin Hood). Neguse was a large and powerful man of thirty-five, experienced in the ways of his world. His reputation stemmed from severe beatings he had given at various times to three men from different families. Furthermore, Neguse seduced the wives of other men, allowed his animals to eat the crops of his neighbors, and claimed use-rights to choice arable land cultivated by other families. These and other bellicose acts made the people of his community fear him. In maintaining his high rank in the community, he continually boasted and verbally assaulted his neighbors with such taunts as, "I shall not worry about you for you are weak." The alliances he had made as a result of his social power caused most people to stand in awe of him. Thus, as otherwise would have been the practice, no one attempted to encroach upon his property or other rights and no one chided him for his breaches of custom.

One family decided to confront Neguse over some of their land recently claimed by him. In a display of might making right, Neguse and ten of his followers began to turn over the disputed land with a plow. The family asked him to stop his plowing, but they were not heeded. Shortly thereafter, the field became one of battle. The family mustered about twenty kinsmen and neighbors who had developed strong resentments of the wielder of the staff and of the mocking tongue. Many of these seekers of vengeance attacked the followers of Neguse, but a good number of them fell upon the main antagonist of their community. In the ensuing fight, repeated heavy blows from the stout staves of his attackers disarmed Neguse and battered him to the ground. When downed, his ribs, arms, and legs were broken by a severe pommeling with sticks and stones, wielded by long-frustrated arms. The followers of Neguse, the *dulaña*, scattered, leaving the broken, nearly lifeless body of their leader oozing blood into the soil he had recently plowed.

"The honor that Neguse took from us made us take *all* honor from him," an elder of the community said afterwards. Neguse is now a shepherd of his kinsmen's livestock, an occupation normally assigned to prepubescent boys, sometimes as young as four years old. With his now atrophied right arm and his limping gait, Neguse, the cripple, has long since recovered as fully as possible from the six months that he was bedridden while his torn body mended. Occasionally, children call to him as they pass saying, "Those people took your power!" Neguse never replies.

What we have just related about Neguse, the shepherd, is not only a case study involving a mechanism of informal social control but is also one concerned with the leveling of social, economic, and other differences in a peasant community. We shall more closely examine this mechanism in the following section on the peasant family, after we first investigate the vertical ties of peasants to an elite of a state.

VERTICAL RELATIONS BETWEEN PEASANTS AND THE WIDER SOCIAL ORDER

Virtually every aspect of a peasant's life is affected to some degree by forces emanating from outside of his home community. These forces are sometimes vertically oriented, frequently involving the direct or delegated social power of the state, of an intrusive foreign state, or of a state-wide religion. More infrequently, the outside force is horizontally oriented and involves the limited social power exercised by another peasant community over some aspect of the activities of the home community. As a peasant community modernizes, the force may become more diffuse as with the economic dynamics of the global market. For instance, the decline of the price of a particular commodity on a distant European exchange may seriously disrupt a community committed to producing it for the world market.

In turning our attention to vertical relationships, we first examine peasant relations with the secular order of the elite. We shall then discuss mediators between the larger society and the peasant community, and, finally, briefly examine peasant relations with the religious order.

Relations with the Wider Secular Order   For purposes of political control, a peasant community is bound vertically to a state through a hierarchy of governmental districts, such as a province and one or more levels of subprovincial units. At times, two or more socially distinct neighboring communities may be united horizontally into the lowest level of governmental district by the elite administrators of the state. Control of peasants by the elite ranges from oppressively firm, as in

France before the revolution, to moderate, as in most of Imperial China, to lax, as in states where central authority is breaking down. The status of peasants under oppressive control may approach slavery, as with European serfs and certain Latin American peons, or actually be slavery, as on many New World plantations and, frequently, during the time of conquest by the elite of a foreign state.

Whether firm or less than firm, the social relations between elite and peasantry range from what may be considered a cultural symbiosis of parasitism to one of mutualism. In the former case, little is given in return for the fund of rent extracted from the peasants, except for some protection against the rent-extracting power of another state. In the latter case, the elite reciprocate with sociopolitical services including public works, such as roads and irrigation systems, aid during "hard times," maintenance of law and order on highways and in the marketplace, and provision for recourse to use of governmental courts for prosecution of criminals and for adjudication of disputes with individuals and the state.

In all instances the state's legal code, an aspect of the Great Tradition, is administered by the literate elite. This code gives legal definition to the status of a peasant, showing him to be subordinate to members of the elite, who "it is written" are superordinate. The superordinate-subordinate relationship is sustained and entrenched by the form of state-regulated tenure of land, through which the peasant-cultivator retains access to arable land and noncultivating peasants retain access to other sites of production. Because of the elite's legal domain over peasants, any local system of land tenure, kinship-based or otherwise, must be validated by state law. Thus, in their subordination, peasant families do not have absolutely inalienable rights to their land, as tribal families may have.

A peasant gives his strongest allegiance to his family and community. The administrative elite of the state are sometimes barely acknowledged and often given only faint support, beyond payment of the fund of rent. In his face to face contacts with the elite, the peasant "plays dumb" in response to questions and requests. This highly adaptive behavior contributes to the outsider's view that peasants are not very bright. (Incidentally, my use of the phrase "play dumb" is taken from the speech patterns of numerous people who migrated from various European peasant settings to the ethnic neighborhoods of my youth. As a boy, when a person with superior power questioned my own or someone else's potentially punishable activity, one of my neighbors would tell me: "Just play dumb. You don't know nothing. You do like I say, and then everything is all right.")

A peasant's strategy related to that of playing dumb is shown in his response to a superior's request for something with an answer approximating, "[Yes, I'll do it] tomorrow." For example, Spanish-speaking peasants say *mañana*, Italians *domani*, Amhara *eshi naga*, and Germans *morgen*; these are all patterned responses of powerless peasants. The "tomorrow" and "playing dumb" behavior exist in part because it is disadvantageous, and sometimes dangerous, to confront a person having superior power with, "No, I won't do it" or, "I won't tell you."

Conscription of a peasant by the state for long-term labor projects and especially to fill the ranks of the army provides close contact for him with government administrators and their subordinates. This contact gives him formal and informal education in appreciation of new ideas, techniques, and artifacts. When a peasant is discharged after army training and returns to his community, he often has greater prestige and abilities of leadership. He may consequently act as an informal agent of change in the community. Furthermore, he often functions as part of an informally organized cadre of local veterans who espouse and extol the policies of modernizing government, especially those of socialistic states which politically educate their soldiers.

Mediators between Peasants and Members of the Elite   Through their knowledge of the ways of the outside world, returning soldiers and other peasants returning from wage labor in the cities contribute to the undermining of certain important and selfishly guarded positions found among many peasantries. The positions existed long before the advent of modernization, which is their undoing, and are occupied by men who may be called cultural "mediators," or "brokers," or "hinges" (cf. Silverman 1965). These middlemen act as links between the local peasant community and outside organizations of agrarian and new elite, of modernized state bureaucracies, and of commerce and industry. A cultural mediator may have, or once have had, a minor governmental, religious, or commercial position, or he may be a lawyer, village teacher, or member of the gentry. Mediators are not always literate, but are wealthier or more "worldly-wise" than the average peasant; they sometimes dwell in town, but then usually have land and kinsmen in the countryside. In return for payment in money, prestige, or obligation, they represent peasants who are insecure in their more involved transactions with representatives of the outside world, for example, with a tax assessor, a commercial agent, or a religious leader above the level of village priest.

Relations with the State-wide and Local Religious Order   State-wide religions unite peasant communities vertically to the state through hierarchical organizations led by a priestly elite, and horizontally to one another through intercommunity ties created by these organizations. Drawing together the peasants of a state into a wider religious order are the universal rites, ideology, and accounts of supernatural beings belonging not just to one community, but innumerable communities embraced by this order. A local aspect of the state-wide order also exists and is epitomized by the community center of worship and activated by localized ritual and holy days.

State-wide religions are bound up with the Great Tradition and administered by the elite; thus they are *for* the peasants but not *of* them. Peasants understand little of the complex written treatises and arcane symbolism of Great Tradition theology. Instead, they verbalize greatly simplified folk, or Little Tradition, versions of this theology. From the peasant viewpoint this Little Tradition version is part of a spectator religion, in which the peasant passively witnesses and only slightly comprehends rites officiated by priests. Practiced alongside this bifurcated religious Tradition is the peasant's participatory religion, which is also a part of his Little Tradition. It is a local supernaturalism existing outside of the ideology and practice of the state-wide bifurcated religion (cf. Buechler and Buechler 1971:94–103; P. Turner 1972:67–72), and for this reason is often proscribed by priests.

The local religious practice has no priests, but may have shamans,[1] magicians,

---

[1] A shaman is a spiritual medium, through whom the spirits speak to man. For further information on kinds of religious practitioners and supernatural beings, and peasant ritual, see Gamst 1969:29–56 and also the unit on religion by Edward Norbeck in this series, Basic Anthropology Units.

Amhara elite of Ethiopia in procession during a national religious holiday in Gondar Town. From right to left: a mounted member of the agrarian secular elite, several of his retainers on foot, a mounted and turbaned member of the clerical elite, and a number of lesser priests and other ecclesiastics.

and diviners, who conduct personalized rites and activities related to local conditions and attuned to personalities and social relations of a particular community. Additionally, peasant families may themselves conduct sacrificial rites to personal, ancestral, and locational spirits with abodes, for example, on nearby hilltops or in bodies of water. In these local practices, a peasant communes directly and in a personally more satisfying way with the supernatural realm, instead of having a conduct-regulating priest stand between him and the spirits.

A syncretism of a peasantry's bifurcated religious Tradition and a local participatory religion is noted in the Buechlers' introduction to the section on manipulation of supernaturalism in their *The Bolivian Aymara*:

> The Aymara attempt to balance the nature/human equilibrium by the judicious manipulation of the supernatural. This balancing manifests itself in certain feasts as well as in magical practices.
>
> Any community member may contribute to the manipulation of the supernatural but often specialists must be called. These belong to two categories, old persons who know how to recite Catholic prayers and fragments of the cathechism and curer/magicians. The former are called for funerals, masses for the dead, All Saints', and the twin ceremony which we shall describe later. They recite prayers as well as direct religious chants. The latter specialists, called *yatiris* or *maestros*, are held in particularly high esteem in the community. As we have mentioned, their opinion carries considerable weight in assemblies. Their position is acknowledged ritually in such ceremonies as the *kachua* when wreaths of bread are placed around their necks. Their prestige is due to the fact that they are indispensable as intermediaries between nature and the supernatural,

a role which they enact vis-a-vis individual community members as well as the section to which they belong as a whole (1971:94).

REACTIONS OF PEASANTRY TO ELITE

Despite the fact that the peasant is subordinated politically and religiously, is tied to the land, must "play dumb," and often needs mediators in dealings with the outside world, he is not absolutely unresponding in his outlook and he will not tolerate limitless demands by the elite. Reactions by peasants against traditional or new elite takes several partially overlapping forms. In these reactions the peasants may attempt to restore a real or imagined social order of the past, a golden yesteryear where present socioeconomic inequities and tribulations did not exist. Or, they may attempt to establish a new social order, a visionary utopia where all men are brothers.

The utopian and yesteryear mythologies of peasants and other folk sometimes focus into a millennarian movement. Originally, movements of this kind supposedly brought about "the millennium," the thousand years of the kingdom of Christ on earth. Hence, by social scientific extension, the millennium is a general time of well-being, beneficial government, and unlimited material good. These movements may remain passive reactions to the agrarian social order, but have been part of many insurrections of peasants. An important example is the so-called "Peasant's Revolt" of peasants and townsmen in Germany during 1524 and 1525 in which the establishment of a new order, Christ's kingdom, was awaited and apparently prepared for by the destruction of cloisters and castles and the killing of secular and religious elite.

Such violent peasant reactions to the elite, whether millennarian-inspired or not, are usually called a jacquerie. This term comes from the name Jacques Bonhomme, which was disdainfully applied by elite to peasants during an insurrection in France during 1358. By extension the term refers to any peasant insurrection. Such uprisings of peasants often stem from increased rates of extraction of the fund of rent, or from attempts to alter the nature of their ties to the land. The jacquerie is usually violent and bloody, but may range to only a display of force without violence. In a fully developed jacquerie, peasants destroy, loot, burn, and kill, often to no long-term avail. In the main, no structural change is effected in the social order of the state, and the peasants are crushed by the elite with a counterreaction of at least equal violence, their grievances going unredressed.

At times, and especially during the past century, governmental agents modify part of their policy in order to vent some of the tension which may lead to or continue a jacquerie. A contemporary example is the moderately violent jacquerie of the Amhara peasants of central Ethiopia in the late 1960s against attempts of the state to change their system of land tenure and related taxation. This insurrection was put down by troops, F–86 Sabre Jets, and some minor concessions on the part of the government.

A much smaller scale insurrection is banditry, when practiced by peasants at least partly as an active reaction against the elite and sometimes the burghers. It is also a way to escape the confines of the poverty of folk life. Although few peasants become full- or part-time bandits, most peasants practice a "psychic insurgency" by revering the careers of past and present folk heroes who successfully defied and robbed those who are socially superior to peasants. Recounting with great satisfaction the exploits of a Robin Hood or a Pancho Villa gives an almost powerless peasant a safe way of publicly expressing hostility toward the elite and their government. Some of the folk heroes are not bandits, but men who simply rebel against oppressive governmental power, for example, William Tell.

Guerrilla insurrection shades into outright banditry on the one hand and into ideological and military resistance on the other hand. "Guerrilla" is derived from a Spanish word meaning "little war"; by extension it refers to warfare conducted by irregular, usually peasant combatants and to these combatants themselves. A guerrilla reaction is sometimes led by a charismatic folk hero, bent upon restoring past conditions or bringing about a new social order. This form of insurrection is not as short-lived and usually not as widespread as the jacquerie. It is more shadowy and submerged into the landscape, hence more protective of its armed peasant insurgents. For this reason a guerrilla reaction is more difficult to suppress than is a jacquerie.

Guerrilla resistance may be against the legitimate government of a state or against the government of an invading state, or both. In either case, the insurrection is against the social order that the domestic or the foreign government embodies. In the example of the Vietnamese guerrillas led by the contemporary folk hero, Ho Chi Minh, not only were foreign political controls being resisted (for example, those of the French and the Japanese), but a new order was also being created to replace older orders (for example, those of the agrarian monarchy and of the superimposed colonial governments). (For concise and penetrating accounts of the Vietnamese insurrection and those of other peasantries during the twentieth century see Wolf 1969.)

Successful peasant revolutions, in which a new social order is founded, as opposed to largely unsuccessful peasant rebellion, in which the old order is only threatened, are a phenomenon of the twentieth century. In the nineteenth century, Karl Marx wrote that even if a peasant participated in a revolution, once he acquired control of a piece of arable land, he would revert back to his customary family-oriented and conservative outlook. Marx knew that peasant values are generally opposed to those of socialism. According to Marx, the revolutionary was going to be the hammer-wielding, urban proletarian and not the sickle-wielding, rural peasant, who had in fact turned his back (cf. Mitrany 1951) on so many urban-spawned rebellions.

In order to lessen any Eurocentric bias to our exemplification of peasant reactions, we should note that insurrections of Chinese peasants have been recurrent events for over two millennia and the majority of these peasant wars were larger in scale than the largest insurrections in medieval Europe (cf. Harrison 1969). One of the more successful peasant insurrections in China began rather disorganized and on a small scale during the late Ming dynasty of the early 1600s (cf. Parsons 1970). The rebellion grew in strength and efficiency of organization until the peasants seized power over large areas of China around 1640 and formed a short-lived government organized on the Imperial model. This peasant government was never strong and a few years after its founding was destroyed by invading warlike pastoralists, the Manchus. The previous Ming government had been weakened in part by years of war with these pastoralists, who were partly acculturated to the Chinese way of life. The Manchus followed the Ming, after the brief peasant interlude, as the last Chinese dynasty until 1912.

As explained by Wolf (1969:276–302), success of insurrections involving peasants during this century results largely from three factors, the first and second of which we regard as significant and the third as all-important. The new social orders created by revolution are partially a result of the recent economic pressures of the monetized global market, which weaken the political ties between traditional elite and peasants and dissolve the social ties uniting peasants to one another. They are also partially a result of the pressures upon land fostered by the rapid population growth accompanying the beginnings of modernization. Despite the significance of these pressures, a disruption of governmental control is necessary before peasant unrest can be channeled into a successful insurrection. Attacks by domestic or foreign forces outside of the peasant sector lead to the breakdown of traditional or modernizing agrarian government (as in Russia during World War I and Yugoslavia, Viet Nam, and China during World War II).

With outside intellectual leadership, initially from the intelligentsia of the urban middle class, peasants are organized and led, as part of an extensive and systematic plan of operation going beyond their traditional poorly organized rebellions, to revolution. In this plan, the peasant sector is given a new millennarian myth for insurrection against the established order. In time, some peasants are trained in the roles of revolutionary and, later, postrevolutionary leadership.

In the case of truly revolutionary new social orders, the peasant is not allowed to reroot himself into his recently liberated plot of cultivable land and to refocus his concern upon his family (as, for example, in China; cf. Buchanan 1970:114–170). Instead, the land is eventually collectivized, and the peasant is given education appropriate to this new situation. Despite the education, the peasant is once again toiling on land he views as not entirely his own. He resentfully sees his production taxed to support a transformed state and its transformed governmental agents. To the peasant, these agents constitute a new elite of impersonal bureaucrats, who are the guardians of a revolutionary version of a little understood social philosophy of a modernizing Great Tradition. His son, or possibly his grandson, will be a postpeasant in a society with a relatively advanced stage of modernization. Perhaps his grandson will be sufficiently educated so that he does not resent his lack of control of his own plot of land and does not resent the extraction of the state's due from his collectivized production. After all, modern techniques of education have a potential to effect, in a generation or two, a radical change in peasant cultural patterns and symbols, even those thought to be "eternal," that is, most deeply rooted in the history of a Little Tradition. The question is, Among how many peasantries will this potential be realized?

6

The Family and Other Social Organizations of Peasants

THE FAMILY IN PEASANT LIFE

In any investigation of the local social organization and relations of a peasant community, it is readily apparent that the family is the basic social unit, of production and exchange, of holding of land and portable property, of ceremonial activity, and of relations in the wider social order. Even in the many peasantries in which larger kinship groups are not important as an organizational basis of society, the kinship-based family group is the focus of most activities for the individual peasant. In addition to the functions just noted, the peasant family, like all human families, has functions that are an institutionalization of mating and paternity and an outlet for sexual drives. It nurtures and provides a social unit of protection for the young, the aged, and the infirm. Finally, in many peasantries the family is the social link between the individual and a larger kinship group, or social structure, through which the individual traces ties of descent, inheritance, and affinity (through marriage).[1]

Using the comparative method on a sample of forty-six communities, Evalyn Jacobson Michaelson and Walter Goldschmidt have arrived at some interesting generalizations on the peasant family. In almost all of the communities, and especially in those with patrilineal families, they find a strong male dominance of family life, which is associated with male control of basic agricultural production (Michaelson and Goldschmidt 1971; Goldschmidt and Kunkel 1971). This dominance derives from the fact that the energies of most male peasants are directed toward cultivation. In contrast to tribalists, they seldom hunt because of the scarcity of game in densely populated peasant areas, and they do not normally engage in warfare because this activity is monopolized by the state. "This argues that the salient ecologic feature of peasant society in formulating the structure of its family life lies in the very existence of the national state in which the peasant community is imbedded" (Goldschmidt and Kunkel 1971:1061).

Additionally, patrilineally organized families emphasize continuity of the patriline

---

[1] Readers desiring additional information on the terms and concepts of the ethnology of kinship explained here and in following passages and footnotes should refer to a work such as Ernest Schusky's *Manual for Kinship Analysis* (1971), his unit on kinship in the series, Basic Anthropology Units, or *Kinship and Marriage* by Robin Fox (Baltimore: Penguin, 1967). See footnotes 2 and 4 of this chapter for systematic presentations of standard terms of kinship used in this chapter and not explained when first introduced, as, for example, the term "patrilineal."

through which land is inherited, and thus have a predominance of arranged marriages serving the interests of family solidarity. In communities with bilateral inheritance marriages are based more upon the choice of the individuals, and there is a lower incidence of reserve between spouses than is the case with patrilineal families. In almost all of the communities surveyed, economic considerations are all important in the choice of a spouse, while romantic love is of little importance (Michaelson and Goldschmidt 1971). After all, a bride and groom do not merely wed one another; they also marry each other's families. Therefore, a very poor or landless peasant finds it difficult to marry one of his children to a more prosperous peasant, no matter how comely and amiable the child may be.

The comparative analysis of the forty-six peasant communities shows three preferred patterns of inheritance of land for this sample. The first and second patterns are invariably associated with a particular family structure, and the third pattern is closely associated with it. These patterns of inheritance are as follows. (1) Patrilineal impartible (not divisible) inheritance of land which is "passed on as a single unit to a single heir" (invariably a son), (2) patrilineal partible inheritance of land, in which all sons may share, and (3) bilateral partible inheritance of land, where "land may be divided among all the offspring, sons and daughters" (Goldschmidt and Kunkel 1971:1061–1062). The particular family structure associated with each of these three patterns is:

> (1) patrilocal stem families, in which a single son continues to reside in the paternal household after marriage, (2) patrilocal joint families, in which all sons continue to reside in the paternal household after marriage, and (3) nuclear families, in which the married offspring establish economically and jurally independent households (Goldschmidt and Kunkel 1971:1062).

To these recent findings we add that marriage generally functions as an alliance between families, and often between the larger kin groups encompassing these families. The peasant family is often an extended one, of three or four generations, but nuclear families, of two generations, are also found. Monogamous marriage is the kind found among peasants in virtually all instances. However, a few cultures allow a man more than one wife, and here we occasionally find polygynous families among wealthier peasants. Very rarely, as among the peasants of Tibet, several men share one wife and thus polyandrous families are found.[2]

As a result of their analysis, Goldschmidt and Michaelson believe that polygyny is not compatible with peasant production and its related dominance by males:

> Among agricultural producers, polygyny is advantageous where two conditions prevail: (1) the women do the bulk of the [cultivation] and (2) land can readily be obtained for successive wives. These conditions make it advantageous on economic grounds for a man to have more than one wife, and plural wives become both a status symbol and an economic asset. These conditions usually prevail under shifting cultivation; they are rarely found in peasant economies (Goldschmidt and Kunkel 1971:1061).

Under pressures resulting from industrialization and the monetized global market, many of the world's peasants are reducing the complexity of their familial organiza-

---

[2] Polygamous families are of two kinds: polygynous, with multiple female spouses, and polyandrous, with multiple male spouses, married to one person of the opposite sex. For explanation of the terms patrilineal and bilateral see footnote 4 of this chapter.

tions to that of the monogamous nuclear family. Some of the specific pressures of modernization involved here are scarcity of land because of recent explosive growth of population, increasing prevalence of wage labor, increasing occupationally specialized divisions of labor in peasant communities, and a growing trend toward cultivation of cash crops for the world market (cf. Wolf 1966:65–73).

LEVELING MECHANISMS AND PEASANT FAMILIES

Each peasant family balances its self-interest against the interests of other families and of its community. Family interests are served openly in situations outside of the community, for example, with attempts to drive a hard bargain in a marketplace or to evade taxes payable to the elite. However, inside the community, family interest must be served carefully or else "corrective action" will be taken by community members. This action is called a leveling, or equalizing, mechanism, which acts to diminish differences in wealth and power.

Leveling mechanisms undoubtedly function to maintain social cohesion and harmony in peasant communities by reducing tensions fostered by socioeconomic inequalities. In these communities, we invariably find different sociocultural, geographical, and situational pressures upon various families, leading inevitably to their socioeconomic differentiation and, consequently, to community tensions relating to disparities in wealth and power between families. Functioning in a way similar to leveling mechanisms are reciprocal mechanisms, particularly those already mentioned concerning production. These act to keep a family from falling into the abyss of unredeemable poverty, and thus level "upward" from poverty, rather than "downward" from prosperity. A suddenly impoverished family can become a disruptive drain on the resources of other families, if it attempts to activate social obligations to it from other families. Thus, by preventing a particular family from falling too low in their economic position, this potential threat to the community is avoided, or at least mitigated.

Of course, a peasant community is not completely egalitarian, despite the related working of these two kinds of social mechanisms. All families are not completely leveled by the mechanisms, which work toward perfect socioeconomic homogeneity and equilibrium, but do not achieve it. Wealthier and more powerful peasant families exist in almost every community. Such families have greater prestige and fill some of the statuses of local secular and religious leadership in the community. The two related mechanisms are probably best exemplified in classic peasant communities, but are also found to varying degrees among those developing into post-peasant communities. Underlying these mechanisms may be an integration of culture approximating the configuration, or ethos, described by George M. Foster with his model, the Image of Limited Good (Foster 1965, 1967). Foster introduces his concept as follows:

> The model of cognitive orientation that seems to me best to account for peasant behavior is the "Image of Limited Good." By "Image of Limited Good" I mean that broad areas of peasant behavior are patterned in such fashion as to suggest that peasants view their social, economic, and natural universes—their total environment—as one in which all of the desired things in life . . . *exist in finite quantity* and *are always in short supply*, as far as the peasant is concerned.

Not only do these and all other "good things" exist in finite and limited quantities, but in addition *there is no way directly within peasant power to increase the available quantities.* It is as if the obvious fact of land shortage in a densely populated area applied to all other desired things: not enough to go around. "Good," like land, is seen as inherent in nature, there to be divided and redivided, if necessary, but not to be augmented (Foster 1965:296).

Whatever the underlying integration of culture, leveling appears to take recurring culturally patterned forms throughout the world. Wolf thinks this leveling is especially apparent in the "closed" rather than in the "open" communities. Comparing closed communities in Java and Mesoamerica, he says:

> In Mesoamerica, display of wealth is viewed with direct hostility. In turn, poverty is praised and resignation in the face of poverty accorded high value. We have seen how much surplus wealth is destroyed or redistributed through participation in the communal religious cult. In Java, there are similar pressures to redistribute wealth:
> . . . every prosperous person has to share his wealth right and left; every windfall must be distributed without delay. The village community cannot easily tolerate economic differences but is apt to act as a leveler in this respect, regarding the individual as part of the community. . . .[3]
> Surplus wealth thus tends to be siphoned off, rather than to be directed towards the purchase of new goods (Wolf 1957:5).

Leveling mechanisms include the sponsoring by a prosperous family of a festive ceremonial occasion, where all members of the community may eat and drink part of the family's wealth (cf. Gamst 1969:83–84). In Mexico, the position of *mayordomo* (steward-sponsor) was often given to a more wealthy peasant. From this position he was required to redistribute a part of his wealth by sponsoring fiestas (cf. Lewis 1960:13–14, 37, 51–52; Vogt 1970:19–22, 78–90).

Although some wealth is leveled when a prosperous family sponsors a festive ceremony, a contravening mechanism is at work simultaneously, for the family's wealth is publicly displayed and its higher rank is publicly validated. Indeed, much of a ceremony that is wholly or partially community-oriented ritually reinforces and acknowledges the differences in rank between peasant families. The goods exchanged between two families when a marriage occurs (cf. Diamond 1969:55–59 and Gamst 1969:106–107) are a very common public display of differences in wealth between families; that is, this exchange is a public exposure of wealth, of which other families may have more or less. Distinctions in rank of peasant families are also evident in highly visible, nonritual contexts, for example, in differences in style and size of houses, in quantity and quality of fields and livestock, and in the value of women's jewelry, especially if it is ostentatiously displayed as among many European peasants.

Leveling is not only manifest in ceremonial and other highly institutionalized ways, but is everpresent in more informal behavior. Such leveling behavior is frequently a reaction against a family's sudden acquisition of wealth, through good fortune or otherwise, and it includes envy, resentful hostility, and suspicion of conduct and motives. These rarely grow into physical abuse but sometimes extend into malicious gossip and verbal abuse and, more commonly, into accusations of

---

[3] Quotation in Wolf from Boeke, 1953.

the use of malevolent supernaturalism. This last is often the neighbors' attribution of a family's good fortune to one of its member's evil acts and thoughts involving supernaturalism, such as communion with a demonic spirit or other practices (see Gamst 1969:39, 44–56).

PEASANT SOCIAL ORGANIZATION BEYOND THE FAMILY UNIT

Familial social structures of peasants, or at times just certain members of these, are organized locally within a community and joined with others horizontally between communities in several ways. These ways are customarily classified by ethnologists into a number of panhuman social organizational principles including kinship and residence. We shall now examine these and other kinds of social organization and the concept of social network in order to comprehend the social ties that unite peasants.

Before we begin our discussion of kinship organization we should note that many educated people who are not ethnologists sometimes find the concepts and terminology of kinship to be rather difficult to understand, sometimes highly esoteric, and often not conducive to the arousal of general interest. Such negative attitudes regarding the ethnology of kinship originate in part in the demise of complex institutions of kinship among the highly industrialized English-speaking peoples, and thus in their (our) first-hand involvement with these institutions. The attitudes are also fostered by the fact that no other discipline studies these institutions; therefore, the average person is unfamiliar with the subject matter and consequently cannot relate it to anything in his previous formal education. The value to the rather unappreciative Westerner of our study of kinship, and the customarily analytically related ritual kinship and small-scale association, is the subject of the introduction to the chapter on the social organization of *The Qemant*:

> The Qemant, like other people of preindustrial regions, are united by a web of kinship not markedly recognized or used in the interactions of industrialized people like the Yankees of North America. In [tribal and most peasant] societies, a person's existence and well-being ultimately depend upon the maintenance of complex links which, when traced through a network of kinship, unite this person with a multitude of relatives. Sometimes, as we shall see among the Qemant, a person with a rather limited kinship network may additionally unite himself with others by fictionalizing kinship links through contracts of reciprocity with those to whom he is otherwise unrelated. Still other Qemant social contracts unite groups of people into associations dedicated to the welfare of members of these groups.
>
> The social organization of the Qemant . . . may, at first glance, seem complex and perhaps even cumbersome. However, the reader should realize that this social organization, like the non-Indo-European language and thought patterns of the Qemant, seems unwieldy to us at first because we are not familiar with it. The Qemant web of kinship is a flexible and economical system of sociocultural elements used to facilitate interpersonal relations. The Qemant kinship network is one of their adaptations to their environment (Gamst 1969:65).

Kinship is usually the organizing principle and the very basis of tribal societies. In the agrarian state, kin ties remain central in the life of the individual peasant (and in the lives of individual nonpeasants). However, as an integrative social network of this complex social order, kinship is secondary, and sometimes even tertiary—for example, in Latin America and India—in importance. As the comparative ethnology of Goldschmidt and Michaelson indicates, kinship organization and kinship-based authority and ethics necessarily become subordinate to the organization, authority, and law of the state, as this kind of social structure becomes fully developed, away from tribalism. Although not the primary social organization, kinship in many peasantries is nevertheless a significant organizing principle. It is to the often still important, but rarely predominant, kinship organization of peasants that we now turn for a comprehensive overview.

KINSHIP ORGANIZATION

Kinship structures may be thought of in terms of networks of social positions, rather firmly organized according to cultural rules of consanguinity (through "blood" relations) and of affinity (through marriage). Extended and nuclear families of peasants are not only the basic social structures of communities, but also of what we call larger kinship groups. Families within these larger structures are united by a network of consanguineal kinship which is organized either cognatically or unilineally.[4] Cognatic systems of kinship are either bilateral or ambilineal, and unilineal systems in almost all instances are patrilineal or matrilineal.

According to the analysis of a sample of forty-six peasantries by Goldschmidt and Michaelson, in contrast to tribal societies most peasant societies do not have larger unilineal kinship groups that are strongly developed in their economic functions. And where these groups exist (as in twenty out of forty-six communities surveyed) they do not allocate rights of land use to families, as they do in tribal societies. Absence or weakness of extended unilineal groups may be accounted for by the existence of the state:

> State authorities tend to be chary of the existence of potentially powerful social units which might form alternative foci of power. In this regard, we are reminded of the ongoing conflict between the Kabakaship [monarchy] in Buganda and the clan organization and of political compromises that this situation entailed. . . . In the measure that the Kabaka failed to assert his ascendancy over the [cultivators] lies the degree to which these rural people failed to be peasants; elsewhere the central political government has succeeded in reducing the effectiveness of the extended kin group as a political and economic force (Goldschmidt and Kunkel 1971:1060).

[4] Two kinds of organization of consanguineal (related by "blood," but actually by genes) kinship have been identified by ethnologists. These are cognatic and unilineal organization. Briefly, cognatic kinship organization is of two kinds. First, it may form groups which include all of an ancestor's descendants, who trace their consanguineal links to him (or her) ambilineally. In ambilineal organization, a person reckons descent to one ancestor through male and female links, but not both links simultaneously in the same generation. Secondly, it may instead form either kin groups (called kindreds) or nongroup networks of kinship, both of which are organized bilaterally. In bilateral organization, a person's ties of consanguineal kinship are traced symmetrically through both sexes to ascending and descending generations. These ties are limited by exclusion of people who are beyond a certain degree of removal in their links of blood relationship. Unilineal kinship organization relates a person consanguineally to males and females through descent links traced either exclusively through father and his male (patri) line (thus through father's father, and father's father's father, and so forth) or through mother and her female (matri) line. The former is called patrilineality and the latter matrilineality.

We now review the functions of larger kinship groups which we hold are rather weakly developed among many, but not all, peasantries. We further note that some peasantries do indeed have strongly developed structures of this kind, some of which do allocate rights to land use, but these structures are invariably subordinated to the state.

Kindreds, the larger kin groups among certain bilaterally organized peoples, are ego-centered and are thus not the same for any kinsmen. Consequently, they are limited in their effectiveness in ordering social relations. They do not exist in perpetuity, coming to an end with the death of the person around whom the kindred is centered. Because they overlap, they create conflicting obligations between kinsmen. Many bilaterally organized peoples do not have kindreds and consequently do not have even the limited kinship grouping in social relations that these provide. Among bilaterally organized peasantries, nonkinship associational principles of local and horizontal organization predominate. Bilaterally organized peasantries are, or were, recently found throughout Latin America, large parts of Europe, and in a few other places such as parts of Southeast Asia.

Patrilineages, matrilineages, and—to a lesser extent—ambilineal descent groups, the larger kinship groups of their respective systems, are far more effective than kindreds in structuring social relations. These groups usually exist in perpetuity as corporate social structures, apart from the births and deaths of their members. Such corporate descent groups regulate the social relations of their members, including most (but sometimes as few as one) of the following activities. The groups regulate marriage and thus forge alliances between families. They may be the local land-holding or land-allocating organization and may also regulate the use of capital goods. They organize mutual aid and other reciprocity between group members and thus foster family security. Additionally, they may adjudicate disputes between group members and may organize religious activities. A good majority of the world's peasants have "lineal" organizations, most of these patrilineal, for example the innumerable Chinese, Arabs, Berbers, Indic- and Dravidian-speaking peoples of India, and the Japanese, to name only a small number of societies. Among peasantries, much rarer than patrilineality is matrilineality, as among the Minangkabau of Indonesia and Malaya, and ambilineality, as among the Amhara of Ethiopia.

The importance of larger kinship groups which are corporate and "lineal" as regulators of social relations has been demonstrated by ethnologists working primarily with tribal peoples. The importance is certainly less among lineally organized peasants, especially where industrialization and the monetized global market have disrupted these groupings of peasants during this century. Nonkinship principles of local and horizontal organization begin to replace kinship principles as these peasants become postpeasants, although the extent of this replacement varies with particular circumstances. Some centuries-old peasantries and some rather recently emerged from tribalism today have great reliance upon an all embracing lineal kin organization of social relations, for example, the Amhara, the Berbers, and the Agaw. Among the Amhara and Qemant Agaw, rights to use land are allocated to heads of families by ambilineal descent groups.

In all, whatever the basis and the degree of importance of a peasant's kinship organization, ties of kinship link him to a network of relatives, not only those living hither and yon in space, but also those across time who are deceased. Spatial and temporal links are used in claiming rights to land, portable property, positions in office, and other desirable prerogatives. The links between living kinsmen unite families in a community, and often in more than one community, for social, economic, religious, political, and other activities.

Although ties of kinship are fundamental and universal in human social organization, limitations exist on the size and complexity of organization and specialization of function supportable by such ties. Larger tribal, agrarian, and industrial societies are necessarily based upon, and all societies contain at least some examples of, various kinds of nonkinship organizations, to which we now turn to understand further the social organization of a peasantry.

NONKINSHIP ORGANIZATION

Nonkinship organization is a category which is a catch-all for a network of social positions based upon principles of social organization other than kinship and residence (to be explained later). One eminent anthropologist calls nonkinship organization a concept that "is merely a convenient lumber room," a residual category of structural odds and ends. We bring order to this messy lumber room by adapting concepts from Paul Bohannan's cogent analysis of the problem of nonkinship organization (1963:144–163) as the basis of our discussion. We should note first that principles of recruitment into nonkinship organization include those of age and, more rarely, sex, for example, the age-graded societies of eastern Africa and men's and the women's "clubs" of societies in Melanesia.

In all societies there are group and nongroup relations whose principle of recruitment is agreement. Agreement has several forms of which two of the most important are contractual, and, of lesser importance, friendship. Friendship is only one of several noncontractual subprinciples of recruitment by agreement to a network of social positions, which in the case of friendship creates enduring social relations. A contract, between two or more people, is an initially voluntary agreement to do or not do a particular thing. The social bond or link between roles which is provided by a contract is definable in terms of the rights and obligations created by the contract. A bond of this kind is not part of another kind of relationship, such as one of kinship or age. Contractual relationships are of two kinds, free and social.

Free, casual contracts provide relations of short duration which are usually non-repetitive. Examples of these are found in an economic exchange between two peasants meeting in a marketplace of a town, or between a clerk and a customer in a department store of an industrial country. The ephemeral relations of free, casual contracts take place in a social network which does not constitute a social group, that is, a network linking two or more people in a to-some-degree enduring relationship.

Social contracts between a number of people provide for the maintenance of a common well-being, or welfare, and are thereby the basis of formal and, often, long lasting groupings of people. These groups range from small-scale, such as those of some tribalists and most folk in which people are associated for purposes of mutual aid—for example, in producing food—to large-scale, such as those of industrial society where groups exist in which people are associated for purposes of production and collective security—for example, the Atchison, Topeka, and Santa Fe Railway Company and the Brotherhood of Locomotive Engineers.

Turning somewhat away from the ideas of Bohannan, but in accord with the terminology of many other anthropologists, we call social contractual groupings "associations." Most societies have "common interest" associations on a small scale (containing more than just a few members), whose functions can have a great range of variation. Small-scale associations are not very important among all peasantries, as for example among the bilaterally organized peasantries of Latin America. However, still smaller dyadic (involving two people) associations are important in this region, as we shall see. Small-scale associations are rare among lineal peasantries of caste-organized India. Robert T. Anderson, a student of peasants and associations, says that traditional peasants and elite generally are organized by territory and kinship. With the growth of states, associations became less important. "As foci of political power, including a degree of pan-tribal influence, their very success [in tribalism] no doubt doomed them. The state imposed its own authority in their place" (1971b:214).

Although generally not as developed among peasants as among industrial and certain tribal peoples, small-scale associations are found in moderately developed forms among some of the world's peasants. Anderson allows that "where the state permits, where circumstances require, and where traditions encourage [association] formation may take place among peasants" (1971b:214). For example, we note that associations are more than moderately developed among the Qemant peasants of Ethiopia (cf. Gamst 1969:58–62, 76–77) five centuries or more after their emergence from tribalism. We additionally note elsewhere in this unit significant peasant associations in Japan, Russia, Java, Mexico, and the Balkans. Associations become more important among modernizing peasants, where ties of kinship begin to atrophy. Finally, we should realize that the state is an extra-large-scale association based upon social contract.

Functions of peasant associations vary greatly, and, as exemplified by Edward Norbeck's study of a Japanese peasant community, may include maintaining community buildings, shrines, and paths, holding festivals, settling interpersonal disputes, banding together against outside pressures—especially from the state—conducting funerals and memorial services, protecting against fire and other chance destruction of property, and cooperating in production and exchange in cultivation and fishing. Still other associational groups are present, including those with educational and police functions (Norbeck 1965:50–54). One of the best known examples of a peasant association is the Balkan *Zadruga*, a grouping by social contract between often otherwise unrelated families, which has the function of cooperative labor and allocation of land. (A popular account of the *Zadruga* is found in Louis Adamic's very readable narrative, *The Native's Return*, and the Zadruga is also featured in the Halperns' case study, *A Serbian Village in Historical Perspective* (1972).) Having mentioned common interest associations, we now focus our attention upon two other important forms of the social contractual, associational organization in peasant life—ritual kinship and the dyadic contract.

Social contract between two or more people is the basis for what ethnologists call ritual, or fictive, kinship. Ritual kinship extends a person's network of consanguineal kinship in accordance with the organizational patterns of this consanguinity; however, the tie that binds is one of ritualized contract rather than of actual consanguinity. Functions and benefits of ritual kinship are approximately those of "real" kinship. Additionally, ritual kinship extends and/or reinforces a familial network of kinship, locally through unions with families in the home community, horizontally with families in neighboring peasant communities, and vertically to rural and urban superiors. Often, fictive children do not acquire rights of inheritance from their fictive parents. This is not always the case, though, as among the Qemant where a fictive child "inherits use rights to land and property from [fictive parents] just like a natural child" (Gamst 1969:74). The incest taboo[5] is frequently extended to fictive kinsmen, as among the Qemant of Ethiopia, but not always, as among their Amhara neighbors.

Ritual parent-child relations and ritual sibling relations, including so-called blood brotherhood, are the most common forms of fictionalized kinship. Reasons for entering into such relations and their functions have already been noted in our passages from Lewis' *Tepoztlan* on the widely studied *compadrazgo* (coparenthood) system of Latin American peasants. Further examples are noted in the Buechlers' *Aymara* (1971:46–49) and in Gamst's *Qemant* (1969:74–75), which also contains a vivid picture of the creation of the ritual bond of fictive kinship called *engohura* (breast child) by the Qemant:

> ... the fictive parent-child relationship was initiated with a minor ceremony in which Ayo and his wife coated their thumbs with honey; the thumbs are said to symbolize the nipples of a woman's breast. Little Zawdu then sucked their thumbs to symbolize his dependency on the couple, who then vowed to act as parents toward their fictive child (1969:74).

What George M. Foster has described (1961, 1963, 1967:212–243) as a dyadic contract, a social relationship binding a pair of individual contractants for certain reciprocities, may also be seen as an example of associational relations. This particular kind of a wide range of dyadic social relations is usually based upon social contract, but may not be, depending upon the circumstances. Dyadic contracts may reinforce links between those already bound by ties of actual or ritual kinship. These contracts appear to be most developed among peasantries where larger lineal kin groups are lacking, as in Latin America, or are breaking down. Foster distinguishes between two kinds of reciprocating dyads. One is the patron-client relation which is vertically oriented and ties a peasant to a more powerful person, usually outside of the comunity, or to a supernatural being. Exchange between the higher and lower statuses is of different kinds of goods and services. The second is the locally or horizontally oriented colleague relation binding peasants (and other folk) of approximately the same socioeconomic status in an exchange of the same kinds of goods and services. Foster's model of dyadic contractual agreements is a valuable construct in the study of modernizing peasantries (and other sociocultural types) where kin and small-scale associational groups are not very well developed or have atrophied.

---

[5] Prohibition of sexual relations between persons united by a link of kinship considered a barrier to these relations.

SOCIAL NETWORK

Social network is a concept of increasing importance in ethnology and should be discussed now that we have mentioned dyadic relations, which are a basic form of networks. Although relatively newly developed in social science, the concept of network (and the overlapping concept of social field) is already confounded with a number of partially conflicting uses and interpretations (see Jay 1964; Swartz 1968; Barnes 1968). The entirety of any society may be thought of in terms of a total network. Such a network consists of a number of interrelated particular networks, or culturally patterned arrangements of social positions. Some parts, or particular arrangements, of a total network are more firmly bounded and some are more amorphously bounded. The former condition predominates in traditional societies and the latter in modernized ones, where enduring groups are not the setting of most social relations.

Kinship and social contractual principles of social organization create human groups rather well bounded spatially and temporally and which thus may be considered as largely firm and stable social networks. In tribal societies and in traditional peasant and pastoral societies, a very large part of the social interaction is organized by these firmly bounded and fully institutionally regulated social networks. In industrial societies kinship, residence, and small-scale associations are no longer of importance in uniting a community, and in modernizing parts of agrarian societies they are of decreasing importance for this purpose. Of course, in no human society, industrial urban or otherwise, are significant social structures totally replaced by amorphous networks. As we have already noted, in industrial society the structures of importance are large-scale contractual associations, but much of its interpersonal relations are of the ephemeral and nonrepetitive free contractual kind.

As a society modernizes more of its interpersonal relations occur in an increasingly amorphous, unstable, and short-lived kind of social organization, often not fully institutionalized and structured. Here, the overlapping of dyadic relations may have little or no functional significance. We may call this kind of social organization an amorphous social network. Amorphous networks not only have no well defined external boundaries but also no clearly demarcated internal units. Parts of modern social networks, amorphous or otherwise, may also be usefully considered as ego-centered personal networks, because virtually everyone in a modernized society has a significantly unique set of social relations. For example, person A has close relations at a place of work with person B, who has close relations in a local beer hall with person C, who does not even know that person A exists.

What we have labeled as an amorphous network is a useful concept for analysis of modernizing or modernized social organizations of peasants. This is especially true when we wish to examine social relations not taking place within or between social structures, such as families, larger kinship groups, associations, and communities. Classic peasants may have some limited amounts of social relations within amorphous networks outside of their traditional structures. Networks of this kind grow and increase in importance as the traditional peasant community becomes one of postpeasants and then of modern agriculturalists. This growth comes about with an increase in strangers visiting the community and in members leaving the community for hours, days, months, or even years, in order to sell their production or labor upon the market. Through amorphous networks, then, community members, and hence the community, may be increasingly linked socially to the outside world. These new amorphous social links greatly expand the scope of peasant relations with the outside, in comparison to the links found within traditional networks of peasant-elite and peasant-townsman social structures and limited amorphous social organization.

As exemplified by peasants migrating to towns and others in urban settings, social relations within amorphous networks may very well be between kinsmen or comembers of a small-scale association (for example, some kind of common interest group), but these ties are not necessary. The social links may be residential, a common territory (such as a city block), or a common former territory (such as a rural "home" community). Most frequent are ties of friendship and free and social contract. These ties are often found in conjunction with shared activities (of work, religion, or leisure) and with interaction because of common backgrounds (such as level of formal education or ethnic group). We close our section on networks by directing the reader's attention to the informative introduction to the subject in the Buechlers' *Aymara* (1971:vii–viii) and to their use of network analysis in the presentation of their data on the Aymara.

RESIDENCE

Residence is a principle of social organization distinct from either kinship or contract. However, residence often overlaps with one of these two nonresidential principles in a group organized by either of them. Associational or kinship groups are by definition mutually exclusive of one another, but neither is necessarily exclusive of residence groups. For example, either nonresidential group may receive its members from people dwelling exclusively in a particular location (thus the principle of residence is also called locality). The basic social unit of the peasant family, and of other cultural types, is primarily a kin group, but it is usually organized secondarily as a residence group. This secondary reinforcement is true of many associational and larger kinship groups of peasants. Thus common residence is always an organizing principle of a peasant community, no matter how it may be cross-cut by kin and associational groups.

Residence is of great importance where we find approximations of Wolf's closed corporate communities (1957). These associational groups are usually organized on the level of an entire community and strongly reinforced by coresidence. Such communities have corporate functions, apart from and enduring beyond the life span of any individual. Functions typically center upon allocation of land, adjudication of disputes, community ceremony, closure of the community to outsiders, and leveling of status distinctions. Some such associationally and residentially organized closed communities may be composed of subunits, for example, the two or more Russian *mirs*, existing in one community. (For a valuable commentary on closed corporateness as a defensive reaction by peasants to a threat from the outside, usually a power-wielding elite, see R. N. Adams 1962:427–430.)

At times, the residential principle may partially divide rather than unify a peasant community. A classic example is found in the residential, or local, moieties among peasants throughout the Islamic Mediterranean region (cf. Murdock 1965). The almost unstudied local moieties occur when a community has two spatially distinct districts. Spatial opposition of the community into two groups is manifest in functions such as rivalry in games and sponsoring of ceremonial occasions. Here, boasting, "one-upmanship," and other covert aggression are present. An important latent function of local moieties may well be as a sort of safety valve for the venting of social and psychic tensions through relatively harmless competition instead of through open disruptive strife, both within and outside of the community (cf. Murdock 1949:90).

7

The Future of Peasants in the Modernizing World

Across the globe today, peasants are being drawn into the vortex of modernization. In this way many are being transformed (depeasantized) as they enter an industrial urban world. This world is optimistically considered by most inhabitants of the affluent North Atlantic countries as the setting from which, through the "magic" of technology, it is possible to increase continually man's standard of consumption, including, eventually, that of the masses of peasants. Social scientists of these countries usually say that because of modernization the disappearance of peasant societies in the not too distant future is inevitable. Such statements are bound up with centuries-old, Western social philosophies concerning "human progress," that is, the inevitability of man's ascent toward ever higher levels of technoeconomic development. A question remains, though. Will all peasants be totally transformed, thus disappearing as such from this earth? Perhaps not for some time to come. Perhaps never.

Current transformation of world peasants can lead to at least four significant end results: (1) capital-intensive urbanism, with occupations including those in industry, commerce, and government; (2) capital-intensive modern agriculture including farming and farming collectivism; (3) largely labor-intensive postpeasant collectivism; and (4) largely labor-intensive postpeasant stabilization. Actually, three or four is a transitional stage to end results one and two, provided that any of a number of interrelated constraints of modernization do not arrest development within three or four to the point that they become end results.

One and two are the dynamic end results of industrial urbanism. These two are interdependent in that rationalized and mechanized modern agriculture reduces manpower requirements and consolidates land holdings as it increases capital costs. Most cultivators thus eventually become surplus labor and are driven from the land to the cities, where they are maintained by nonagricultural occupations or government welfare. Three takes the form of collectivized agricultural communities, directly controlled by government, in which the cultivator loses his familial ties to the land. He is not yet fully a farming collectivist, but is still a peasant in much of his behavior and outlook. Postpeasant collectivism is a radically different kind of postpeasantry, and we therefore distinguish it from the postpeasantry where familial ties to the land remain during modernization. Postpeasant collectivism is found principally in revolutionary programs of modernization of peasants with an associated centralization of authority, for example, in Communist states such as China, and elsewhere, as in some parts of Mexico and several Arab states. Four is found in more gradual programs of modernization with less centralized authority, as in most of the politically unaligned and economically underdeveloped states of the "Third World," for example, India and much of Mexico. As may be seen in Mexico, three and four are not mutually exclusive in any one country.

It is possible that all peasants can reach the interrelated first and second end results and become transformed into modern types. However, it is also possible that large parts of the peasantries of many countries will be arrested in their transformation and remain at the third or fourth end result, thus perpetuating to varying degrees many of the patterns of culture attributed to them in this book. A very strong argument in support of the likelihood of this perpetuation is furnished by development in the Soviet Union. Despite half a century of rapid modernization, the USSR still has almost one-half of its population living in rural communities, where only ten percent of the agricultural production is fully mechanized and most cultivation is "still done by primitive manual techniques" (Alexander Vucinich's "Foreword" to Dunn and Dunn 1967). This population is still being slowly transformed from folk to industrial urbanite and to modern agriculturalist with an increasingly urban culture. In the Soviet Union, with its vast industrial and geographic wealth, transformation of peasants into industrial urban modernity will undoubtedly be completed early in the next century. But a question still remains. What about modernization of the rest of the world, those areas that are not so well-endowed and did not have an early start in the "race" for industrialization of nonagricultural and agricultural production?

We begin our discussion of this question with the observation that the earth's physical resources are finite, constituting not just a situation of limited material good, but one of diminishing good of nonrenewable resources, for example, metallic ores and fossil fuels (cf. Meadows et al. 1972:54–69). Given the finiteness of earthly resources, including the fossil fuels and products of agriculture energizing present-day technologies, which also have inherent limits to increases in productivity, we note the following consequence. As the industrialized thirty percent of mankind, consuming eighty percent of the world's energy, leaps forward to attain increasingly higher levels of unprecedented material affluence, a corresponding increasingly smaller limit is effected in the number of people the earth can support with life styles above privation. Although the "pie" of material resources may be politically redivided, this pie cannot be increased in size. (An exception would be an increase, through a still emerging nuclear technology, in the bare trace of energy now released by this means—in the United States, about one-third of one percent of the country's total energy supply. However, the cost and the rate of development and application of the elements of a Nuclear Power Revolution currently allow little likelihood of nuclear energy "saving" the Third World in the eleventh hour.)

Therefore, during the 1970s, because of a lack of sufficient developmental resources, it may no longer be possible to modernize fully all peasants (who constitute over one-half the world's population). Scarcity of resources is aggravated by the destructive effects of industrial pollution upon our habitat and its material wealth. This contention that the earth may no longer be able to sustain modernization of peasants—and, of course, other folk and tribal peoples—is supportable in a number of related ways, upon which we now expand.

First of all, several rather Jeremian but reasonable socioeconomic studies (including Forrester 1971; Meadows et al. 1972) hold that even with the inclusion of hypothetical "technological miracles," all projections of growth for industrial states end in their collapse. Not only is the present level of consumption in the West unequaled in the history of man, but it may be unattainable in the future. With continuation of present developmental trends, industrialized states may be non-sustainable and perhaps even self-extinguishing.

According to one of the latest of these recent studies (Meadows et al. 1972: 163–164): (1) consumption of resources must be cut drastically to one-quarter of 1970 levels, (2) population growth must be reduced to zero, and (3) output of industrial capital must only slightly exceed present levels. Enforcement of the first requirement is almost politically untenable in the affluent Western democracies (and perhaps also in near affluent Communist Europe). For much of mankind, attainment of the second requirement is politically impossible and socially unacceptable at present, even if the necessary contraceptive resources could be distributed to this end. Finally, even a partial enforcement of the third requirement undermines whatever chance remains for modernization of basically agrarian states and hence of their masses of peasants. Realistically, this requirement would amount to the ultimate neocolonialism.

If we reject the increasingly more prevalent Jeremian studies as too severe in their projections, we come up against a somewhat related barrier to modernization of agrarian states. The scarce resources necessary for transformation of peasants into our first and second end results are controlled by those countries which modernized first. For example, the industrially pioneering United States with six percent of the world's population consumes forty percent of its physical resources, both to sustain its modernized nature and to sate its inhabitants' material hunger. Necessary for support of large-scale modernization of have-not countries would be a program in the United States (and other industrialized countries) for redistributing some of its wealth and relinquishing control of a large part of its overseas resources to these countries. A program of this kind is politically unacceptable in the United States, especially when its consequences are envisioned—only half a chicken in every pot and no car in the garage (which will not stand empty since it will probably have to be used for housing). Even if implemented somehow, a program of this kind would probably be one of "too little, too late," considering the effects of the "exploding" population of have-not states.

Why do not the underdeveloped lands "make it on their own," just as the industrialized countries did? This query is answerable historically. Modernization of Euro-American "primary" industrial states was a slow process, spanning at least two centuries. This process had financially and technologically modest stages at the beginning. These stages are not possible for have-not states attempting to enter the financially and technologically advanced condition of today's modernity. Witness the debacle of the home-made blast furnaces in peasant villages during China's consequently retrograde Great Leap Forward of the late 1950s. As part of its beginnings of modernization, the West subjugated and exploited most of the world both as a source of raw materials, bullion, labor, and other resources, and as a marketplace of supportive consumers for its nascent manufacturing, transportation, and commercial enterprises of joint stock capitalism. Subjugation and exploitation were rationalized and facilitated by a variety of forms of racism practiced by Europeans. Developing states today are not able to underwrite the costs of modernization in these ways.

Instead, modernization of most have-not countries is supported in the main by the peasant sector of these basically agrarian societies. Peasants pay for modernization directly in the form of taxes on their land and agricultural and other production. They also pay for it indirectly by providing a self-maintaining pool of cheap, seasonal and permanent labor for development, by providing a dumping ground for inferior goods and services of a protected developing industry, and by constituting a sector of society which can be neglected in the providing of socioeconomic services (such as education, public health, and transportation) by a government with meager resources. Through these direct and indirect ways capital is accumulated for investment in development. Where peasants work for government on collective farms, they usually receive small compensation, thus leaving more of their production for allocation to state projects of modernization. Even when the small surplus extracted directly and indirectly from a peasant family is multiplied by that from many millions of such families, it is usually not sufficient to purchase an appreciable amount of the scientifically and technologically advanced industry necessary for modernization in today's world. This is especially so if capital goods, raw materials, and technical services must be extensively imported for a particular industrial project. As industrial technology continues an exponential rate of increase in its development, and therefore its cost, slight agrarian surpluses allow purchase of still less industrialization.

Runaway population growth, whose global doubling rate is presently twenty-eight years and constantly decreasing, also lessens the amount of industrialization that can be purchased. Where an exploding population of a basically agrarian state consumes almost all increases in gross national product in the form of bread, its capacity for self-development with domestic means is nil. Present-day foreign aid is not much help either, because half of it is in the form of guns and the other half very often has the effect of someone giving an aspirin to a man with a spreading cancer. Frequently, as in the case of Pakistan during 1971, the guns are used for shooting insurgent peasants. Sometimes, as in Venezuela during recent years, the guns are used by governments of modernizing states to shoot insurrectionary folk who would nationalize local nonrenewable resources of development, which are controlled by the all-consuming, fully industrialized countries. And, still more detrimental to modernization, even if military aid and sales to agrarian governments are not used to suppress social change initiated by peasants, they represent scarce resources diverted away from development. Even in the few cases where population growth does not devour all or almost all gains in national productivity, the rate of industrialization is rarely sufficient to provide employment for either the growing rural or urban populace.

With slow industrialization, those peasants who do migrate to town because of demographic pressure on the land come to largely preindustrial centers which offer little opportunity for steady employment. A peasant's new status as townsman gives him in return a home consisting of a mat or two in the gutter of a teeming city or a few sheets of scrap material fastened together in a sprawling and festering shanty-slum. Nutrition in these mushrooming urban settings is commensurate with the wretchedness of the domiciles.

Presently mushrooming cities of developing agrarian states are growing at a disconcerting rate, far outstripping the rate of urbanization of modernizing Euro-America in the nineteenth century. According to Kingsley Davis:

> Today the underdeveloped nations—already densely settled, tragically impoverished and with gloomy economic prospects—are multiplying their people by sheer biological increase at a rate that is unprecedented. It is this population boom that is overwhelmingly responsible for the rapid inflation of city populations in such countries. Contrary to popular opinion both inside and outside those countries, the main factor is not rural-urban migration (1965:50).

Davis continues:

> Given the explosive overall population growth in underdeveloped countries, it follows that if the rural population is not to pile up on the land and reach an economically absurd density, a high rate of rural-urban migration must be maintained. Indeed, the exodus from rural areas should be higher than in the past. But this high rate of internal movement is not taking place, and there is some doubt that it could conceivably do so.
>
> The poor countries thus confront a grave dilemma. If they do not substantially step up the exodus from rural areas, these areas will be swamped with underemployed cultivators. If they do step up the exodus, the cities will grow at a disastrous rate (1965:51).

Thus current urban growth is not, in most cases, draining significant numbers of peasants off the land thereby permitting a lowering of the labor intensity of cultivation. Consequently, agriculture remains traditional in part because it is not economical to replace very much of the inexpensive peasant labor on their small plots with costly modern agricultural techniques and capital. Without replacement of labor-intensive, traditional cultivation with expensive modernized agriculture, peasants' lifeways—which partially result from traditional technology and from relatively dense, rural population—will persist, even if in modified form. A government controlled, partially modernized agriculture allowing increase in crop production while maintaining a dense rural population using labor-intensive techniques is sometimes advocated as the solution to the world food and population problems. Such a solution would contribute to the maintenance of peasantries.

The explosion of peasant and urban populations in developing countries is caused by the recent Public Health Revolution of declining mortality, underwritten to a large extent by the industrial resources of the West. This earthshaking revolution has greatly diminished the effect of the age-old major control of human population growth—the microbiological part of the environment. Even simple modern efforts to improve public health lead to radically reduced rates of infant mortality and of death before the time of old age.

Thus, the severest of the interrelated limitations upon transformation of peasant into industrial urbanite or modern agriculturalist is unplanned and unchecked population growth. Overcrowded rural peasants of states with slowly industrializing and teeming cities are the heritage of such population growth. This growth is all the more pernicious in its effects when it is coupled to other conditions of under-

Movement of logs with elephant power in Ceylon. Replacement of this and other work animals of agrarian society with fuel-energized machines necessitates prohibitively costly additions to a developing state's industrial and commercial infrastructure.

development already mentioned. Clearly, birth control would seem to be an answer to alleviating the misery of poverty in developing countries. But, even if this control is somehow attainable to a degree sufficient for the easing of privation, it is probably not attainable to a degree sufficient for the accumulation of enough capital for full modernization in the foreseeable future.

Neo-Malthusian theories advocating control of population growth are rejected by some Third World planners. For example, Josué de Castro (1967), a renowned authority on problems of hunger, is instead in favor of programs of agrarian and marketing reform as the means to eradicating hunger and its social concomitants. But does an agronomic alternative to birth control exist for developing countries? "Scientific miracle projects" for increasing production of food, from "farming the sea" to the much heralded "green revolution" with its high-yield grains, may not keep pace with exploding population (cf. Borgstrom 1972). Indeed, the green revolution may not be applicable to all developing areas, since it is based upon the costly use of both chemical fertilizers and relatively large amounts of water which usually must be pumped with fuel energized machines from specially constructed tube wells.

Furthermore, agricultural production beyond certain limits necessitates multiple cropping with swift harvesting and replanting. This agricultural technique requires tractors and other fuel energized machines (and repair shops with trained mechanics, facilities for distribution of petroleum supplies and spare parts, factories for manufacturing tractors, oil refineries, tire factories dependent upon synthetic rubber works using 2500 tons of water to manufacture one ton of rubber, and so on). A national infrastructure including, among other things, far more extensive systems of agricultural credit, marketing, storage, and transportation must also be developed (with the insufficient resources available). This development is necessary to extend the green revolution away from the limited, easily "revolutionized" areas that are geographically and socioeconomically favorable to agricultural modernization (for example, India's Punjab region), to the more widespread, less favorable areas. Without extension of this kind, the current attempt at agrarian development will not be truly revolutionary in its contribution to modernization and to the transformation of peasants. In many developing countries the green revolution has relatively little effect on much of the capital-poor peasantry. For example, in Mexico during the 1950s, one of the earliest phases of the green revolution, eighty percent of the increase in agricultural output came from just three percent of the units of cultivation; in this case all were highly capitalized farms (Shaw 1970:44).

To sum up our discussion of restraints upon transformation of peasants, we note the following. Increasing demographic pressure, lack of sufficient natural resources, scarcity of international developmental capital, the exponentially increasing constraints of industrial pollution of the geographical environment, global hunger, and other restrictions of modernization all interrelate to create conditions which tend to maintain a labor-intensive peasant sector throughout much of the world. Because of exploding population and lack of sufficient capital for industrialization, urbanization of have-not countries cannot adequately accommodate those who are already urbanites, let alone absorb peasants into the urban fold. Thus, population pressure mounts on arable land (and even labor-intensive peasantries begin to experience underemployment on the land). Even if capital and natural resources necessary for development were furnished to the populous have-nots by the haves, modernization most likely would eventually be slowed and then arrested by the physical limits on the availability of the earth's natural resources and ability to absorb the pollution concomitant to industrialization. In support of these contentions, we further note what the ecologist George Borgstrom wrote recently on the subject of the restraints of modernization, after he extensively reviewed recent literature on modernization and its ecological setting:

> The explosive trend in population numbers shows few signs of abatement. The gap in food, water and other of life's necessaries has widened rather than narrowed. Almost no advances have been made toward a greater equity in availability of foods and other raw materials. A favored minority of the human family is, like the last Bourbons, holding on to their privileges and grabbing an unreasonable portion of the world's riches, and this in order to sustain a civilization so shortsighted and wasteful that it cannot serve as a pattern to a world in misery and parsimony.
>
> In effect, man threatens to deprive himself of a future by refusing to recognize his predicament. Insanely we try to talk ourselves out of reality. We refuse to acknowledge the rising human tidal wave. We profess to believe that our civilization will be the first in history to attain immortality. We are convinced we know the secret of perpetuating our way of life with the aid of science and technology. Yet our fate is to be read as in an open book (1972:vii–viii).

To answer our original question, then, let us begin by expressing the hope that the Jeremian ethnology presented in this chapter is proven wrong during the remainder of the twentieth century. However, numerous and strong indications exist that the global depeasantizing transformation is "running out of fuel" and slowing and may eventually stabilize in much of the world. Accordingly, peasants will probably be around longer than some social scientists envision. One last comment: With unchecked continuation of present trends in industrial growth and the consequent exhausting of nonrenewable resources such as metallic ores, industrial civilization may well collapse, ending not with a thermonuclear bang but with a whimper. In such an eventuality, postpeasantries will not only "be around longer," but will also constitute the supportive sector of the brave new postindustrial civilization.

Questions for Discussion

1. Under what sociocultural and geographical conditions did peasant society originate? How does control of energy relate to the origin, stabilization, and modernization of peasantries?
2. According to the material presented in this book, what are "folk"? In what ways do they contrast to tribalists and industrial peoples?
3. In what ways are reciprocity and redistribution characteristic of Yankee society?
4. What are the differences and similarities between the life style of a farming family and a classic peasant family?
5. What may we say about the effect of the state on greater kinship groups and upon associational groups in peasant society?
6. Discuss examples of a "cultural lag" in values apropos of rural cultivators being maintained in urban areas by the laws of your state/province/country.
7. Explain how peasant families tend to level differences toward a middle rank and tend to balance interests of the family against those of the community. Support your explanation with ethnographic data from the Case Studies in Cultural Anthropology or from other ethnographies on peasants.
8. Despite schisms and hostile interpersonal relations found between peasant families, counteracting social mechanisms and organizations fostering community solidarity are at work. Discuss this statement with data from the Case Studies in Cultural Anthropology or from other ethnographies on peasants.
9. Examine novels on peasant life and agrarian society and analyze and discuss their contents with the ideas and facts presented in this book. Suitable novels coming readily to mind include: Pearl Buck's *The Good Earth* (a study of a Chinese peasant family with innovating sons and a tradition-bound father), Ignazio Silone's *Fontamara* (a drama of Fascist-induced change in a "timeless" Italian village), Mikhail Sholokhov's *And Quiet Flows the Don* (a literary masterpiece of world war, revolution, and civil war in the land of the Don Cossacks), Giovanni Verga's *The House by the Medlar Tree* (an aristocrat's novel of a Sicilian fishing village), and Guiseppe di Lampedusa's *The Leopard* (a tale of the decline of a family of agrarian elite in post-Risorgimento Italy).
10. In what ways is the study of peasant culture and society of value for an informed person in today's world?
11. How does the ethnologist study peasant culture and society? (See the Studies in Anthropological Method listed in Chapter 1 for further information needed in an extensive consideration of ethnological methods and techniques of research.)
12. Explain how the concept of the state and its social power as developed in this book is useful for an understanding of peasant life.
13. What is meant by the phrase, the increasing urbanization of the industrial world?
14. Discuss the importance of writing to an understanding of peasantry. What do the concepts of Great and Little Tradition have to do with this understanding?
15. Burghers facilitate the modernization of agrarian society in what ways?
16. Compare the techniques of horticulture with those of agriculture as practiced by peasants.
17. Market exchange in traditional peasant economies may be characterized as small-scale. Explain.
18. What are the major effects of the monetized global market upon classic peasant life?
19. Market exchange is not solely related to the marketplace, and the marketplace has functions other than exchange. Explain.
20. What is ritual kinship? Illustrate your answer with data from the *compadrazgo* system of Mexico.

21. What is the *jajmani* system of India? How could it affect present-day modernization in India?
22. Cultural mediators play what role in many peasant societies, and what is their fate in a modernizing state?
23. The various forms of peasant reaction against elite examined in this book are similar and different in what ways? Give examples of these reactions from novels, poetry, folk tales, and folk songs.
24. Among peasantries with a corporate lineal organization, what might the relationships be between the family and the larger kinship group?
25. What is the range of associational organization among peasants? Give examples in your discussion using the concept of social contract.
26. Social network is a concept of increasing importance in social science. How is it useful in the study of peasants? Are all social networks bounded in the same way?
27. Explain the relationship between kinship, associational, and residential groupings. What aspects of peasant societies may be usefully viewed as residentially organized?
28. With your knowledge of current and recent events across the globe, what do you think is the future of the world's peasantries? Read the studies of modernization listed in the References and Recommended Reading and the reviews of these works in the various social scientific journals (for example, the *American Anthropologist* and the *Journal of Developing Areas*), then discuss this question again. Have your views changed? If so, what led to this change?
29. Should and could Western peoples curtail their standard of consumption in order to aid in the development of the world's have-nots? What are the socioeconomic implications of such a curtailment for you, your family, and your community?
30. Read the works by de Castro, Ehrlich, Fanon, and Worsley listed in the References and Recommended Reading. Then decide if birth and population control constitute an answer to world poverty. If so, whose answer?
31. While demanding abatement of pollution by our industry, may we demand equally that developing agrarian states transfer a significant fraction of their meagre industrial resources from development to abatement of pollution? Now that "we have ours" may we request a change in the rules of the game of development? (Under the "old rules," the cost of industrialization is underwritten in part by polluting the environment.) What happens to global ecological balances if 800 million Chinese and 500 million Indians "modernize" to the point where they pollute at the rate of 200 million Yankees?

References and Recommended Reading

Listed here and marked by asterisks are the references cited in this book. Also listed are additional items recommended to further stimulate and guide the student in his study of peasants and their place in the modern world. Case Studies in Cultural Anthropology are marked CSCA.

*Adams, Richard N., 1962, "The Community in Latin America: A Changing Myth." *The Centennial Review* 6:409–434.

*Adams, Robert McC., 1966, *The Evolution of Urban Society: Early Mesopotamia and Prehispanic Mexico.* Chicago: Aldine.

*Adamic, L., 1934, *The Native's Return: An American Immigrant Visits Jugoslavia and Discovers His Old Country.* New York: Harper & Row.

Anderson, Robert T., 1965, "Studies in Peasant Life." In B. J. Siegel, ed., *Biennial Review of Anthropology 1965.* Stanford, Calif.: Stanford University Press, pp. 176–210.

*——, 1971a, *Traditional Europe: A Study in Anthropology and History.* Belmont, Calif.: Wadsworth.

*——, 1971b, "Voluntary Associations in History." *American Anthropologist* 73: 209–222.

Apter, David, 1965, *The Politics of Modernization.* Chicago: University of Chicago Press.

Banton, Michael, 1964, "The Folk Society and Civilization." *Race* 6:27–33.

*Barnes, J. A., 1968, "Networks and Political Process." In M. J. Swartz, ed., *Local Level Politics.* Chicago: Aldine, pp. 107–130.

Bates, Daniel G., 1971, "The Role of the State in Peasant-Nomad Mutualism." *Anthropological Quarterly* 44:109–131.

*Beals, Alan, 1962, *Gopalpur: A South Indian Village.* New York: Holt, Rinehart and Winston. CSCA.

*Beattie, John, 1965, *Understanding an African Kingdom: Bunyoro.* New York: Holt, Rinehart and Winston.

Beqiraj, Mehmet, 1966, *Peasantry in Revolution.* Ithaca, N.Y.: Center for International Studies, Cornell University.

Bock, Philip K., ed., 1969, *Peasants in the Modern World.* Albuquerque: University of New Mexico Press.

*Boeke, J. H., 1953, *Economics and Economic Policy of Dual Societies: As Exemplified by Indonesia.* New York: Institute of Pacific Relations.

*Bohannan, Paul, 1963, *Social Anthropology.* New York: Holt, Rinehart and Winston.

*Borgstrom, Georg, 1972, *The Hungry Planet: The Modern World at the Edge of Famine,* 2d ed. New York: Macmillan.

Bottomore, T. B., 1966, *Elites and Society.* Baltimore: Penguin.

Brokensha, David, and Charles Erasmus, 1969, "African 'Peasants' and Community Development." In D. Brokensha and M. Pearsall, eds., *The Anthropology of Development in Sub-Saharan Africa,* Society for Applied Anthropology Monograph No. 10:85–100.

Brown, Lester R., 1970, *Seeds of Change: The Green Revolution and Development in the 1970's.* New York: Praeger.

*Buchanan, Keith, 1970, *The Transformation of the Chinese Earth.* London: G. Bell.

*Buechler, Hans C., and J.-M. Buechler, 1971, *The Bolivian Aymara.* New York: Holt, Rinehart and Winston. CSCA.

*Castro, Josué de, 1967, *The Black Book of Hunger*. Boston: Beacon.

Chaliand, Gérard, 1969, *The Peasants of North Vietnam*. Baltimore: Penguin.

*Chayanov, Alexander V., 1966, *The Theory of Peasant Economy*, D. Thorner et al., eds. Homewood, Ill.: Irwin.

*Childe, V. Gordon, 1951, *Man Makes Himself*. New York: New American Library.

*Cole, Sonia, 1970. *The Neolithic Revolution*. London: British Museum.

*Collier, John, Jr., 1967, *Visual Anthropology: Photography as a Research Method*. New York: Holt, Rinehart and Winston.

*Coon, Carleton S., 1958, *Caravan: The Story of the Middle East*. New York: Holt, Rinehart and Winston.

*Dalton, George, 1971, *Economic Development and Social Change*. Garden City, N.Y.: Natural History Press.

*————, 1972, "Peasantries in Anthropology and History." *Current Anthropology* 13:385–415.

*Davis, Kingsley, 1965, "The Urbanization of the Human Population." *Scientific American* 213(3):41–53.

————, 1972, "The Changing Balance of Births and Deaths." In H. Brown and E. Hutchings, Jr., eds., *Are Our Descendants Doomed? Technological Change and Population Growth*, New York: Viking.

*Derman, Bill, 1972, "Peasants: The African Exception? Reply to Goldschmidt and Kunkel." *American Anthropologist* 74:779–782.

*Diamond, Norma, 1969, *K'un Shen: A Taiwan Village*. New York: Holt, Rinehart and Winston. CSCA.

*Dunn, Stephen P., and Ethel Dunn, 1967, *The Peasants of Central Russia*. New York: Holt, Rinehart and Winston. CSCA

*East European Quarterly, 1970, 4:237–367 (whole issue), "Anthropology in East-Central and Southeast Europe."

Ehrlich, Paul R., 1968, *The Population Bomb*. New York: Ballantine.

————, and Anne H. Ehrlich, 1970, *Population, Resources, Environment: Issues in Human Ecology*. San Francisco: Freeman.

Erasmus, Charles J., 1956, "Cultural Structure and Process: The Occurrence and Disappearance of Reciprocal Farm Labor." *Southwestern Journal of Anthropology* 12:444–469.

————, 1967, "Upper Limits of Peasantry and Agrarian Reform: Bolivia, Venezuela, and Mexico Compared." *Ethnology* 6:349–379.

*Fallers, L. A., 1961, "Are African Cultivators to Be Called 'Peasants'?" *Current Anthropology* 2:108–110.

Fanon, Frantz, 1965, *The Wretched of the Earth*. New York: Grove.

* Fél, Edit, and Tamás Hofer, 1969, *Proper Peasants*. Chicago: Aldine.

Firth, Raymond, 1950, "The Peasantry of South East Asia." *International Affairs* 26:503–514.

Fitchen, J. M., 1961, "Peasantry as a Social Type." In *Symposium: Patterns of Land Utilization and Other Papers*. Proceedings 1961 Annual Spring Meeting, American Ethnological Society. Seattle: University of Washington Press.

*Forrester, Jay Wright, 1971, *World Dynamics*. Cambridge, Mass.: Wright-Allen.

*Foster, George M., 1953, "What Is a Folk Culture?" *American Anthropologist* 55:159–173.

————, 1960–1961, "Interpersonal Relations in Peasant Society." *Human Organization* 19:174–184.

*————, 1961, "The Dyadic Contract: A Model for the Social Structure of a Mexican Peasant Village." *American Anthropologist* 63:1173–1192.

*————, 1962, *Traditional Cultures: And the Impact of Technological Change*. New York: Harper & Row. (Second edition 1973)

*————, 1963, "The Dyadic Contract in Tzintzuntzan, II: Patron-Client Relationship." *American Anthropologist* 65:1280–1294.

*————, 1965, "Peasant Society and the Image of Limited Good." *American Anthropologist* 67:293–315.

*————, 1967, *Tzintzuntzan: Mexican Peasants in a Changing World*. Boston: Little, Brown.

————, 1972, "The Anatomy of Envy: A Study in Symbolic Behavior." *Current Anthropology* 13:165–202.

Franklin, S. H., 1962, "Reflections on the Peasantry." *Pacific Viewpoint* 3:1–26.

————, 1969, *The European Peasantry: The Final Phase*. London: Methuen.

*Fraser, Thomas M., Jr., 1966, *Fishermen of South Thailand: The Malay Villagers*. New York: Holt, Rinehart and Winston. CSCA.

Friedl, Ernestine, 1963, "Studies in Peasant Life." In B. J. Siegel, ed., *Biennial Review of Anthropology 1963*. Stanford, Calif.: Stanford University Press, pp. 276–306.

Fromm, Erich, and Michael Maccoby, 1970, *Social Character in a Mexican Village*. Englewood Cliffs, N.J.: Prentice-Hall.

*Gamio, Manuel, ed., 1922, *La Plolación del Valle de Teotihuacán*, Tomo I, II, III. Mexico, D. F.: Dirección de Talleres Graficos.

*Gamst, Frederick C., 1969, *The Qemant: A Pagan-Hebraic Peasantry of Ethiopia*. New York: Holt, Rinehart and Winston. CSCA.

*————, 1970, "Peasantries and Elites without Urbanism: The Civilization of Ethiopia." *Comparative Studies in Society and History* 12:373–392.

Geertz, Clifford, 1962, "Studies in Peasant Life." In B. J. Siegel, ed., *Biennial Review of Anthropology 1961*. Stanford, Calif.: Stanford University Press, pp. 1–41.

————, 1968, "Village." *International Encyclopedia of the Social Sciences* 16:318–322.

*Goldschmidt, Walter, and Evalyn J. Kunkel, 1971, "The Structure of the Peasant Family." *American Anthropologist* 73:1058–1076.

*Goody, Jack, 1968, "Introduction." In J. Goody, ed., *Literacy in Traditional Societies*. Cambridge: At the University Press, pp. 1–26.

*————, and Ian Watt, 1963, "The Consequences of Literacy." *Comparative Studies in Society and History* 5:304–345.

Halpern, Joel M., and John Brode, 1967, "Studies in Peasant Life." In B. J. Siegel and A. R. Beals, eds., *Biennial Review of Anthropology 1967*. Stanford, Calif.: Stanford University Press, pp. 46–139.

*Harrison, James P., 1969, *The Communists and Chinese Peasant Rebellions: A Study in the Rewriting of Chinese History*. New York: Atheneum.

*Henry, Frances, and Satish Saberwal, eds., 1969, *Stress and Response in Fieldwork*. New York: Holt, Rinehart and Winston.

Hobsbawm, E. J., 1959, *Primitive Rebels: Studies in Archaic Forms of Social Movement in the 19th and 20th Centuries*. Manchester: Manchester University Press.

Hoselitz, Bert F., 1960, *Sociological Aspects of Economic Growth*. New York: Free Press.

*Hsu, Francis L. K., 1969, *The Study of Literate Civilizations*. New York: Holt, Rinehart and Winston.

Huizer, Gerrit, 1970, "'Resistance to Change' and Radical Peasant Mobilization: Foster and Erasmus Reconsidered." *Human Organization* 29:303–322.

Hunter, Guy, 1969, *Modernizing Peasant Societies: A Comparative Study in Asia and Africa*. London: Oxford.

*Jay, Edward, 1964, "The Concepts of 'Field' and 'Network' in Anthropological Research." *Man*, No. 177.

Jeffries, Sir Charles, 1967, *Illiteracy: A World Problem*. New York: Praeger.

Johnson, Chalmers A., 1962, *Peasant Nationalism and Communist Power*. Stanford, Calif.: Stanford University Press.

————, 1964, *Revolution and the Social System*. Stanford, Calif.: The Hoover Institution.

Johnson, Douglas L., 1969, *The Nature of Nomadism: A Comparative Study of Pastoral Migrations in Southwestern Asia and Northern Africa*. Department of Geography Research Paper No. 118. Chicago: University of Chicago Press.

*Kroeber, A. L., 1947, "Culture Groupings in Asia" *Southwestern Journal of Anthropology* 3:322–330.

*——, 1948, *Anthropology.* New York: Harcourt Brace Javanovich.

Krader, Lawrence, 1953, "The Cultural and Historical Position of the Mongols." *Asia Major* 3:169–183.

——, 1968, "Pastoralism." *International Encyclopedia of the Social Sciences* 11: 453–461.

Kushner, Gilbert, 1970, "The Anthropology of Complex Societies." In B. J. Siegel, ed., *Biennial Review of Anthropology 1969.* Stanford, Calif.: Stanford University Press, pp. 80–131.

*Langness, L. L., 1965, *The Life History in Anthropological Science.* New York: Holt, Rinehart and Winston.

*Lewis, Oscar, 1960. *Tepoztlán: Village in Mexico.* New York: Holt, Rinehart and Winston. CSCA.

*——, and Victor Barnouw, 1956, "Caste and the Jajmani System in a North Indian Village." *Scientific Monthly* 83(2):66–81.

Löffler, Reinhold, 1971, "The Representative Mediator and the New Peasant." *American Anthropologist* 73:1077–1091.

Lopreato, Joseph, 1965, "How Would You Like to Be a Peasant?" *Human Organization* 24:298–307.

*Lundberg, Ferdinand, 1968, *The Rich and The Super-Rich.* New York: Bantam.

*McNeill, William H., 1963, *The Rise of the West.* Chicago: University of Chicago Press.

Mangin, William, ed., 1970, *Peasants in Cities: Readings in the Anthropology of Urbanism.* Boston: Houghton, Mifflin.

*Marriott, McKim, 1955, "Little Communities in an Indigenous Civilization." In M. Marriott, ed., *Village India: Studies in the Little Community.* American Anthropological Association, Memoir No. 83:171–222.

*Meadows, Donella H., et al., 1972, *The Limits of Growth: A Report for the Club of Rome's Project on the Predicament of Mankind.* New York: Universe Books.

Meier, Gerald M., 1970, *Leading Issues in Economic Development,* 2d ed. London: Oxford.

*Michaelson, Evalyn J., and Walter Goldschmidt, 1971, "Female Roles and Male Dominance among Peasants." *Southwestern Journal of Anthropology* 27:330–352.

*Mitrany, David, 1951, *Marx against the Peasant: A Study in Social Dogmatism.* Chapel Hill: University of North Carolina Press.

*Murdock, George P., 1949, *Social Structure.* New York: Macmillan.

*——, 1965, "Political Moieties." In G. P. Murdock, *Culture and Society.* Pittsburgh: University of Pittsburgh Press.

*Norbeck, Edward, 1965, *Changing Japan.* New York: Holt, Rinehart and Winston. CSCA.

*Parsons, Elsie Clews, 1936, *Miltla, Town of the Souls.* Chicago: University of Chicago Press.

*Parsons, James B., 1970, *The Peasant Rebellions of the Late Ming Dynasty.* Tucson: University of Arizona Press.

*Pelto, Pertti J., 1970, *Anthropological Research: The Structure of Inquiry.* New York: Harper & Row.

Peristiany, Jean G., ed., 1966, *Honor and Shame: The Values of Mediterranean Society.* Chicago: University of Chicago Press.

*Polanyi, Karl, 1957, "The Economy as Instituted Process." In K. Polanyi et al., eds., *Trade and Market in Early Empires.* Glencoe, Ill.: Free Press and The Falcon's Wing Press.

Potter, Jack M., M. N. Diaz, and G. M. Foster, eds., 1967, *Peasant Society: A Reader.* Boston: Little, Brown.

*Redfield, Robert, 1930, *Tepoztlán, A Mexican Village: A Study of Folk Life.* Chicago: University of Chicago Press.

*———, 1940, "Introduction." To Horace Minor, *St. Dennis: A French Canadian Parish*. Chicago: University of Chicago Press, pp. xiii–xix.

———, 1941, *The Folk Culture of Yucatan*. Chicago: University of Chicago Press.

*———, 1947, "The Folk Society." *American Journal of Sociology* 52:293–308. [Originally published in 1942.]

*———, 1953a, "The Natural History of the Folk Society." *Social Forces* 31:224–228.

*———, 1953b, *The Primitive World and Its Transformations*. Ithaca, N. Y.: Cornell University Press.

*———, 1955a, "The Social Organization of Tradition." *The Far Eastern Quarterly* 15:13–21.

———, 1955b, *The Little Community*. Chicago: University of Chicago Press.

*———, 1956, *Peasant Society and Culture*. Chicago: University of Chicago Press.

———, and Milton Singer, 1954, "The Cultural Role of Cities." *Economic Development and Cultural Change* 3:53–77.

*Sahlins, Marshall D., and Elman R. Service, 1960, *Evolution and Culture*. Ann Arbor, Mich.: University of Michigan Press.

*Sauer, Carl O., 1952, *Agricultural Origins and Dispersals*. New York: American Geographical Society.

Schusky, Ernest L., 1971, *Manual for Kinship Analysis*, 2d ed. New York: Holt, Rinehart and Winston.

*Scientific American, 1971, 224(3) (whole issue), "Energy and Power."

*Service, Elman R., 1971, *Cultural Evolutionism: Theory in Practice*. New York: Holt, Rinehart and Winston.

Shanin, Teodor, 1966, "The Peasantry as a Political Factor." *The Sociological Review* 14:5–27.

———, 1971, *Peasants and Peasant Societies: Selected Readings*. Baltimore: Penguin.

*Shaw, Robert d'A., 1970, *Jobs and Agricultural Development*. Washington, D.C.: Overseas Development Council.

*Silverman, Sydel F., 1965, "The Community-Nation Mediator in Traditional Central Italy." *Ethnology* 4:172–189.

*Singer, Milton, 1972, *When a Great Tradition Modernizes: An Anthropological Approach to Indian Civilization*. New York: Praeger.

Sjoberg, Gideon, 1952, "Folk and 'Feudal' Societies." *American Journal of Sociology* 58:231–239.

*———, 1960, *The Preindustrial City: Past and Present*. Glencoe, Ill.: Free Press.

*Spindler, George D., ed., 1970, *Being an Anthropologist: Fieldwork in Eleven Cultures*. New York: Holt, Rinehart and Winston.

*———, 1973, *Burgbach: Urbanization and Identity in a German Village*. New York: Holt, Rinehart and Winston. CSCA.

*Swartz, Marc J., 1968, "Introduction." In M. J. Swartz, ed., *Local-Level Politics*. Chicago: Aldine, pp. 1–46.

Thorner, Daniel, 1968, "Peasantry." *International Encyclopedia of the Social Sciences* 11:503–511.

*Turner, Paul R., 1972, *The Highland Chontal*. New York: Holt, Rinehart and Winston. CSCA.

*Turner, Ralph E., 1941, *The Great Cultural Traditions: The Foundations of Civilizations*, 2 vols. New York: McGraw-Hill.

*Vogt, Evon Z., 1970, *The Zinacantecos of Mexico: A Modern Maya Way of Life*. New York: Holt, Rinehart and Winston. CSCA.

*Weingrod, Alex, 1969, "Cultural Traditions in Developing Societies: Great, Little & Mass." In P. K. Bock, ed., *Peasants in the Modern World*. Albuquerque: University of New Mexico Press, pp. 99–108.

Wheatley, Paul, 1963, " 'What the Greatness of a City Is Said to Be': Reflections on Sjoberg's 'Preindustrial City.' " *Pacific Viewpoint* 4:163–188.

———, 1969, "City as Symbol." An inaugural lecture delivered at University College, London, 20 November, 1967. London: H. K. Lewis.

*White, Leslie A., 1949, "Energy and the Evolution of Culture." In Leslie A. White, *The Science of Culture.* New York: Grove, pp. 363–393.

*———, 1959, *The Evolution of Culture: The Development of Civilization to the Fall of Rome.* New York: McGraw-Hill.

*Williams, Thomas R., 1967, *Field Methods in the Study of Culture.* New York: Holt, Rinehart and Winston.

Wolf, Eric R., 1955, "Types of Latin American Peasantry: A Preliminary Discussion." *American Anthropologist* 57:452–471.

*———, 1957, "Closed Corporate Peasant Communities in Mesoamerica and Central Java." *Southwestern Journal of Anthropology* 13:1–18.

*———, 1966, *Peasants.* Englewood Cliffs, N. J.: Prentice-Hall.

———, 1967, "Understanding Civilizations: A Review Article." *Comparative Studies in Society and History* 9:446–465.

*———, 1969, *Peasant Wars of the Twentieth Century.* New York: Harper & Row.

*———, 1972, "Commentary on George Dalton, 'Peasantries in Anthropology and History'." *Current Anthropology,* 13:410–411.

Worsley, Peter, 1970, *The Third World,* 2d ed. Chicago: University of Chicago Press.

Case Studies of
Peasant Communities*

Alan R. Beals, 1962, *Gopalpur: A South Indian Village*. Gopalpur is a small village located in South India. The case study includes information on childhood and its consequences; family and kin; Jati and village links; religion; and conflict and its resolution.

Hans C. Buechler and Judith-Maria Buechler, 1971, *The Bolivian Aymara*. This case study focuses on Compi, a community on the shores of Lake Titicaca on the Bolivian High Plateau. Compi is viewed as a part of a complex system with reference to wider social, temporal, and spatial framework. The authors have applied the concept of social networks in the analysis of interpersonal interaction. The case study includes substantial coverage of the economic organization and its changes, as well as the fiesta system and a system of sponsorship called Cargo, which is widespread in Latin America.

Norma Diamond, 1969, *K'un Shen: A Taiwan Village*. K'un Shen is a fishing village on the island of Taiwan. Its inhabitants are descendents of seventeenth- and eighteenth-century migrants from southeastern China. Their way of life represents one of the significant variants of traditional Chinese peasant culture. Special attention is given to the economic basis of life, which is largely sea fishing done close to shore, but this is supplemented by fish ponds that are owned and cultivated by individual households. Also included are chapters on child rearing; family, household, and lineage; and religious life.

Stephen P. Dunn and Ethel Dunn, 1967, *The Peasants of Central Russia*. This study gives students an ethnographic description of significant aspects of Russian peasant life. It is based on secondary sources in Russian written by Soviet ethnographers. Chapters on the Kolkhoz village and family, education and social mobility, folk institutions, and material culture are provided.

Hani Fakhouri, 1972, *Kafr el-Elow: An Egyptian Village in Transition*. Kafr el-Elow is eighteen miles south of Cairo situated in the midst of one of the most densely populated agricultural areas in the world. It is now undergoing rapid industrialization and urbanization. The village and its area have, therefore, become characterized by sharp contrasts in almost every dimension of life. These contrasts and changes are a constant theme of the case study, which describes the economy, family and kinship system, religion, government, and education.

Thomas M. Fraser, Jr., 1966, *Fishermen of South Thailand: The Malay Villagers*. This is a study about the people of Rusembilan who are Muslims and this and other features which distinguish them from the rest of Thailand in a culture area oriented towards Malaysia. The author gives an analysis of the compartmentalization of values resulting from the influence of Islam superimposed on a traditional Malay Southeast Asian culture of long standing, which in turn is influenced by Thai culture. The analysis shows how the internal integration of the village is declining due to certain technological changes which have directly affected the allocation of roles and statuses in the community.

Ernestine Friedl, 1962, *Vasilika: A Village in Modern Greece*. This study shows how land resources, cotton cultivation, division of labor, concepts of cleanliness and order, the furnishing of homes, the dowry system, and ceremonies and festivities interrelate so that a patterned way of life as a whole emerges. The reader acquires

---

* From the Case Studies in Cultural Anthropology, edited by George and Louise Spindler and published by Holt, Rinehart and Winston, Inc.

insight into the quality of interpersonal relationships in Vasilika, which, like those between man and nature, are characterized by constant struggle. Special attention is given to the dowry and inheritance system.

Frederick C. Gamst, 1969, *The Qemant: A Pagan-Hebraic Peasantry of Ethiopia.* The Qemant speak a dialect of the Cushitic language and practice a religion composed of syncretized Pagan and Hebraic elements with a few Christian features. The Qemant are of special interest as an example of a peasantry unaffected by modernization and as an example of acculturation brought about by other than Euro-American culture. The Qemant are being Amharized, not Westernized.

Joel M. Halpern and Barbara Halpern, 1972, *A Serbian Village in Historical Perspective.* This case study provides historical perspective for the community called Orasac and yet deals with changes concomitant with modernization. It places Orasac in the context of the larger national whole. Special attention is given to the *Zadruga* and its social system ramifications. The *Zadruga* is a basic social unit in Serbian peasant life and deserves serious analysis. Careful attention is also given to resources, economy and changing occupations, the life cycle, ritual life, and current cultural change.

Michael M. Horowitz, 1967, *Morne-Paysan: Peasant Village in Martinique.* This case study is about an inland agricultural village in Martinique, an island of the West Indies. The treatment includes a detailed discussion of household composition, a matter of special interest in Caribbean ethnology; an analysis of agriculture and markets; a discussion of factions and conflicts within the village as related to religion, economics, and politics; and a description of the round of life from birth to death. The present situation of Morne-Paysan is seen as a derivative of colonization, emancipation, and industrialization. Significant processes are dealt with, such as the prolitarianization of the peasantry, that are occurring throughout the Caribbean.

Michael Kearney, 1972, *The Winds of Ixtepeji: World View and Society in a Zapotec Town.* This study deals with the world view and socialization of the Zapotec town of Ixtepeji in the state of Oaxaca, Mexico. The world view is represented by five basic propositions through which the author expresses underlying motivations prevailing in the system and in turn relates these to the structural context. The study is therefore in the framework of cognitive anthropology, as the author continually asks, "How do the people perceive their situation?" Although world view is the focus, other salient features of the cultural and social system are dealt with and interrelated, such as politics, economics, and religion. The author also describes how the current world view, patterns of social interaction, farming practices and technology, and attitudes about the landscape and its resources are obstacles inhibiting economic and social development.

Oscar Lewis, 1960, *Tepoztlán: Village in Mexico.* This is a case study of the Mexican village Tepoztlán placed on a timeline that extends from the tenth century A.D. and the Toltec Empire to the present; from legendary history to contemporary anthropological observation. The main focus is upon how life is lived today in the village, which is typical of many others inhabited by Mexican peasants. Economics, intrafamilial relationships, and the life cycle are described. The last chapter provides a vivid account of change as Tepoztlán acquires electricity, new roads, and buses—all harbingers of more sweeping changes to come as the village of the Mexican peasant adapts to the impact of urbanization and industrialization.

John C. Messenger, 1969, *Inis Beag: Isle of Ireland.* The people of Inis Beag are widely known through journalism and film. The author makes clear why the image of the people, embedded as it is in a context of romanticism and nativism, scarcely approximates reality. The picture that emerges is less heroic than the current romanticized idealization, but it is a very human one. It is an analysis of a closed community that provides mobility only by migration. Special attention is given to the influence of puritanism, which in a context of Catholicism is particularly interesting. The case study is also characterized by a strong focus on Irish folklore, Christian reinterpretations of pagan elements, music, song, and dance. Subsistence, material culture, social organization, social control, values, and religion are also covered. An historical introduction in the context of relevant aspects of Irish history is provided.

Joe E. Pierce, 1964, *Life in a Turkish Village*. This case study provides a picture of life in an Anatolian village as seen through the eyes of a small boy just beginning the long induction into a man's role. A more conventional analysis of Anatolian village life is also provided with descriptive interpretations of the social system, economy, political structure, religious and folk beliefs, and language and world view.

George D. Spindler, 1973, *Burgbach: Urbanization and Identity in a German Village*. This is a study of the confrontation of the past and the future in a village in southern Germany, one of the many in Europe and elsewhere in the world where dramatic urbanization and industrialization are taking place and a traditional folk community is being overwhelmed by modernization. Special attention is given to cultural persistence of strivings for identity, the mutual adaptation of migrant newcomers and natives to ritualization and the effects of rationalization, and the effect of the school and its culture upon children who must adapt to an environment foreign to their teachers and parents.

Paul R. Turner, 1972, *The Highland Chontal*. This study provides an excellent account of the Chontal Indian system laid out in a modern componential manner and explicitly compared to that of the United States. The book is organized in terms of social, cultural, and personality systems. A section on cultural change provides a useful perspective on the implications of purposeful cultural change by cultural agents of a different cutlural system from that of the people whose behavior is being changed.

Evon Vogt, 1970, *The Zinacantecos of Mexico: A Modern Maya Way of Life*. This case study focuses on the ways that ritualization and ceremonialism interpenetrate all aspects of life in Zinacantan, one of twenty-one Tzotzil-speaking Indian *municipios* in the Highlands of Chiapas, located between the Isthmus of Tehuantepec and the Guatamalan border. The Zinacantecos' cultural system is of special interest since it has endured the change from independence before the European invasion to status as a conquered people; as well as Christian-Catholic proselytizing. Chapters are provided on the Zinacantecos' universe, the ceremonial center and the hamlets, the social cycle, the economic cycle, the life cycle, the ritual cycle, and a short chapter of particular interest on replication in both structural and conceptual dimensions.

George and Louise Spindler
The Editors